Solo Slow Cooking Effortless One Person Meals with Easy Steps

⬅—————————➡

Vibrant Photos Attached Original Flavor Tested Recipes

By Diana Stone

Copyright © by Diana Stone

All rights reserved. No part of this publication may be reproduced, distributed, or transmitted in any form or by any means, including photocopying, recording, or other electronic or mechanical methods, without the prior written permission of the publisher, except in the case of brief quotations embodied in critical reviews and specific other noncommercial uses permitted by copyright law. This book is protected by copyright laws and treaties worldwide, and the unauthorized reproduction of this work may lead to legal proceedings.

The content of "Solo Slow Cooking: Effortless One-Person Meals with Easy Steps," including texts, graphics, recipes, and images, is the property of Diana Stone and is protected by copyright and other intellectual property laws. The collection of recipes within this book are original creations that have been meticulously developed and flavor-tested to ensure authenticity and satisfaction for every home cook.

This book has been published by the rules and regulations of Kindle Direct Publishing (KDP) and is subject to KDP's terms of service. The following features characterize this book:

- ✓ It comprises 50 uniquely crafted recipes tailored for solo dining, making it perfect for individuals seeking the convenience and comfort of slow cooker meals.
- ✓ The book comprises five thematic chapters: Meat, Chicken, Vegetarian, Fish & Seafood, and Snacks, each containing 10 recipes.
- ✓ Every recipe has been authentic and cooked initially, accompanied by vibrant, colorful photos that illustrate the finished dish, providing a visual guide to complement the easy-to-follow instructions.
- ✓ The book is printed in standard color for the paperback edition, enhancing each page's visual enjoyment and appeal.
- ✓ Special care has been taken to ensure that the recipes are easy to follow, ideally tested for flavor, and presented without any grammatical or spelling errors.

For permissions, requests, or further inquiries regarding the reproduction or use of any material from this book, please get in touch with the publisher directly. This book is designed to offer accurate and authoritative information regarding the subject matter covered, with the understanding that the author and publisher are not providing professional culinary advice.

Introduction

Welcome to "Solo Slow Cooking: Effortless One-Person Meals with Easy Steps," a culinary journey curated by Diana Stone, designed exclusively for the solo diner who seeks the simplicity and comfort of slow-cooked meals without the fuss. This cookbook is a celebration of the joy of cooking for oneself, offering a collection of 50 recipes that cater to individual tastes and preferences, all while ensuring that each meal is as delightful to prepare as it is to savor.

A Culinary Adventure for One

Embark on a unique culinary adventure that respects your time and taste buds. "Solo Slow Cooking" is your guide to exploring a world of flavors, textures, and aromas with the ease and convenience of a slow cooker. Each recipe has been meticulously crafted, tested, and perfected to ensure you enjoy authentic, flavorful meals every time you dine.

Diverse and Delightful Recipes

The book is thoughtfully divided into five chapters—Meat, Chicken, Vegetarian, Fish and Seafood, Soup—each featuring 10 original recipes. Whether you're in the mood for a hearty meat dish, a light vegetarian meal, a savory seafood creation, or a comforting soup, "Solo Slow Cooking" has something special just for you.

Vibrant Visuals and Flawless Flavors

Every recipe comes with vibrant, original photos that showcase the finished dish and serve as a visual guide through the cooking process. The standard color printing enhances these images, making each page a feast for the eyes and inspiring you to recreate these delicious meals in your kitchen.

Designed for Ease and Excellence

"Solo Slow Cooking" prides itself on its easy-to-follow instructions, ensuring that even those new to slow cooking can achieve perfect results. The book has been rigorously edited to be free from grammatical or spelling errors, allowing you to focus entirely on the joy of cooking.

Diana Stone invites you to embrace the art of slow cooking with "Solo Slow Cooking: Effortless One-Person Meals with Easy Steps." This cookbook is more than just a collection of recipes; it's a companion for those evenings spent in your own company, celebrating the simplicity and satisfaction of cooking for oneself. Prepare to be delighted by the flavors, nourished by the meals, and inspired by the ease with which you can create them. Welcome to your new favorite way to dine solo.

Table of Contents

Chapter 01: Solo Meat Feasts 7
Recipe 01: Slow Cooker Beef Brisket 7
Recipe 02: Slow Cooked Veal Stew 9
Recipe 03: Slow Cooker Beef Stew 11
Recipe 04: Nalli Nihari Lamb Stew with Rice 13
Recipe 05: German Wagyu Beef Roulades 15
Recipe 06: Lamb Curry 17
Recipe 07: Slow Cooker Thick and Chunky Beef Stew 19
Recipe 08: Home Made Stew and Dumplings 21
Recipe 09: Cannellini Beans Beef Stew 23
Recipe 10: Baby Back Ribs 25

Chapter 02: Chicken for One 27
Recipe 11: Chicken Taco with Corn 27
Recipe 12: Shredded Chicken in Cream Cheese Sauce and Bacon ... 29
Recipe 13: Crack Chicken Over Egg Pasta 31
Recipe 14: Chicken with Seasoning Mix 33
Recipe 15: Peanut Chicken 35
Recipe 16: White Chili Chicken with Beans 37
Recipe 17: Chicken Vegetable Stew 39
Recipe 18: Barbecue Chicken Wings 41
Recipe 19: Thai Red Chicken Curry 43
Recipe 20: Tex-Mex Chicken Stew 45

Chapter 03: Vegetarian Delights 47
Recipe 21: Stewed Cabbage Potato 47
Recipe 22: Chickpea, Broccoli, Carrot Curry Cooked in Coconut Milk 49
Recipe 23: Pumpkin Lentil Curry and Rice 51
Recipe 24: Vegan Lentil Soup 53
Recipe 25: Butternut Squash 55

Recipe 26: Vegetable Ratatouille 57

Recipe 27: Carrot Potatoes Green Beans 59

Recipe 28: Dal Makhani 61

Recipe 29: Minestrone Vegetable Soup 63

Recipe 30: Mushroom Vegan Lentil Stew 65

Chapter 04: Seafood Solo 67

Recipe 31: Slow Cooker Salmon Risotto 67

Recipe 32: BBQ Shrimp 69

Recipe 33: Fish Curry with Mango 71

Recipe 34: Octopus Salad 73

Recipe 35: American Fish Stew 75

Recipe 36: Spanish Seafood Paella 77

Recipe 37: Italian Seafood Pasta 79

Recipe 38: Hake Stew with Potatoes 81

Recipe 39: Italian Risotto 83

Recipe 40: Seafood Risotto with Mussel Shrimp and Squid 85

Chapter 05: Snackable Moments 87

Recipe 41: King Ranch Chicken Soup 87

Recipe 42: Mexican Fiesta Chicken Soup 89

Recipe 43: Mushroom Soup 91

Recipe 44: Lentil Spinach Soup 93

Recipe 45: Split Pea Turkey Soup 95

Recipe 46: Meatball Vegetable Soup 97

Recipe 47: Ham and Cannellini Bean Soup 99

Recipe 48: Split Pea Bacon Soup 101

Recipe 49: Tuscany Sausage Gnocchi Bean Soup 103

Recipe 50: Sweet Potato Split Pea Soup 105

Chapter 01: Solo Meat Feasts

Recipe 01: Slow Cooker Beef Brisket

This hearty slow cooker beef brisket, complemented by a fresh coleslaw and the aroma of thyme, is a delightful one-person meal that combines ease with elegance.

Servings: 1

Cook Time: 6 hours

Prepping Time: 20 minutes

Difficulty: Medium

Ingredients:

- 250g beef brisket
- 1/2 cup beef broth
- 1 tbsp olive oil
- 1 tsp fresh thyme
- 1/2 tsp garlic powder
- Salt and pepper to taste
- 1 cup shredded cabbage
- 1 tbsp mayonnaise
- 1 tsp white vinegar
- 1/2 tsp sugar

Step-by-Step Preparation:

1. Rub the brisket with olive oil, thyme, garlic powder, salt, and pepper.
2. Place the brisket in the slow cooker and add beef broth.
3. Cook on low for 6 hours until tender.
4. Mix cabbage with mayonnaise, vinegar, sugar, salt, and pepper for the coleslaw.
5. Let the coleslaw chill in the refrigerator.
6. Once the brisket is done, slice it and serve with chilled coleslaw.

Nutritional Facts: (Per serving)

- Calories: 650
- Protein: 48g
- Carbohydrates: 15g
- Fat: 45g
- Sodium: 650mg

This slow cooker beef brisket with coleslaw and thyme is perfect for those seeking a satisfying, no-fuss dinner. Its tender meat and crisp coleslaw will surely delight your taste buds.

Recipe 02: Slow Cooked Veal Stew

Savor the rich flavors of slow-cooked veal stew, perfectly combined with potatoes and carrots, for a comforting, single-serving meal that warms the soul.

Servings: 1

Prepping Time: 15 minutes

Cook Time: 8 hours

Difficulty: Easy

Ingredients:

- 200g veal, cubed
- 1 medium potato, diced
- 1 large carrot, sliced
- 1 onion, chopped
- 2 cloves garlic, minced
- 1 cup beef broth
- 1 tsp tomato paste
- 1/2 tsp dried thyme
- Salt and pepper to taste

Step-by-Step Preparation:

1. Place the veal cubes in the slow cooker.
2. Add the diced potato, sliced carrot, chopped onion, and minced garlic.
3. Pour in the beef broth and stir in tomato paste.
4. Season with dried thyme, salt, and pepper.
5. Cover and cook on low for 8 hours until the veal is tender and the vegetables are cooked.
6. Adjust seasoning if necessary and serve hot.

Nutritional Facts: (Per serving)

- Calories: 500
- Protein: 35g
- Carbohydrates: 45g
- Fat: 20g
- Fiber: 6g
- Sodium: 700mg

This slow-cooked veal stew with potato and carrot offers a wholesome, delicious escape into culinary comfort. Its tender, flavorful bites provide the perfect end to any day.

Recipe 03: Slow Cooker Beef Stew

Indulge in the comforting embrace of a classic slow cooker beef stew tailored for a delightful single-serving meal that satisfies your cravings with its rich flavors and tender beef.

Servings: 1

Prepping Time: 15 mins

Cook Time: 7 hrs

Difficulty: Easy

Ingredients:

- 200g beef chuck, cubed
- 1 small potato, diced
- 1 carrot, sliced
- 1/2 onion, chopped
- 1 garlic clove, minced
- 1 cup beef broth
- 1 tbsp tomato paste
- 1/2 tsp dried rosemary
- Salt and pepper to taste

Step-by-Step Preparation:

1. Place the cubed beef in the slow cooker.
2. Add diced potato, sliced carrot, chopped onion, and minced garlic.
3. Pour in beef broth and add tomato paste.
4. Season with dried rosemary, salt, and pepper.
5. Cover and cook on low for 7 hours until the beef is tender.
6. Stir well before serving, adjusting seasoning if needed.

Nutritional Facts: (Per serving)

- Calories: 520
- Protein: 36g
- Carbohydrates: 40g
- Fat: 25g
- Fiber: 5g
- Sodium: 700mg

This slow cooker beef stew is a hearty, homemade meal, offering a perfect blend of savory beef and vegetables. It's an ideal choice for a cozy, no-fuss dinner experience.

Recipe 04: Nalli Nihari Lamb Stew with Rice

Immerse yourself in the rich flavors of Indian cuisine with Nalli Nihari, a slow-cooked lamb stew infused with aromatic spices and served alongside fluffy rice. Perfect as a luxurious single-serving meal, this dish is a testament to the art of slow cooking.

Servings: 1

Prepping Time: 25 mins

Cook Time: 8 hrs

Difficulty: Moderate

Ingredients:

- 200g lamb shank (Nalli)
- 1/2 cup basmati rice
- 1 small onion, finely chopped
- 2 cloves garlic, minced
- 1-inch piece ginger, grated
- 1 tbsp Nihari spice mix
- 2 cups water
- 1 tbsp ghee (clarified butter)
- Salt to taste
- Fresh cilantro for garnish

Step-by-Step Preparation:

1. Sauté onion, garlic, and ginger in ghee until golden.
2. Add the lamb shank, Nihari spice mix, and salt; stir well.
3. Transfer to a slow cooker and add water.
4. Cook on low for 8 hours until the lamb is tender.
5. In a separate pot, cook basmati rice according to package instructions.
6. Serve the Nihari over rice, garnished with fresh cilantro.

Nutritional Facts: (Per serving)

- Calories: 600
- Protein: 40g
- Carbohydrates: 50g
- Fat: 25g
- Fiber: 4g
- Sodium: 620mg

Enjoy this Nalli Nihari with rice as a sumptuous treat, bringing the essence of Indian slow cooking to your dining table, perfect for a cozy and indulgent meal.

Recipe 05: German Wagyu Beef Roulades

Indulge in a gourmet fusion of German cuisine with this exquisite dish of Wagyu beef roulades, accompanied by spaetzli and draped in a spicy gravy sauce. Crafted for a luxurious single serving, this recipe brings a touch of elegance to your slow cooker repertoire.

Servings: 1

Prepping Time: 30 mins

Cook Time: 6 hrs

Difficulty: Advanced

Ingredients:

- 1 Wagyu beef slice (150g), thinly pounded
- 1/4 cup spaetzli
- 1 small carrot, finely chopped
- 1/4 onion, finely chopped
- 1 garlic clove, minced
- 1/2 cup beef broth
- 1 tbsp tomato paste
- 1 tsp paprika
- Salt and pepper to taste
- 1 tbsp olive oil

Step-by-Step Preparation:

1. Sauté carrot, onion, and garlic in olive oil until softened.
2. Spread this mixture on the beef slice, roll tightly, and secure with toothpicks.
3. Place the roulade in the slow cooker.
4. Mix beef broth, tomato paste, paprika, salt, and pepper; pour over the roulade.
5. Cook on low for 6 hours.
6. Prepare spaetzli as per package instructions.
7. Serve the roulade with spaetzli and drizzle with the spicy gravy.

Nutritional Facts: (Per serving)

- Calories: 650
- Protein: 40g
- Carbohydrates: 35g
- Fat: 35g
- Fiber: 3g
- Sodium: 680mg

This German Wagyu beef roulade with spaetzli in spicy gravy sauce presents a luxurious and flavorful journey, perfect for a special evening when you wish to treat yourself to an exquisite, slow-cooked delight.

Recipe 06: Lamb Curry

Discover the rich and aromatic flavors of traditional Lamb Curry, a slow cooker dish that perfectly blends tender lamb with a symphony of spices. Ideal for a solo dinner, it's a culinary journey to the heart of comforting flavors.

Servings: 1

Prepping Time: 15 mins

Cook Time: 6 hrs

Difficulty: Medium

Ingredients:

- 200g lamb, cut into chunks
- 1 small onion, diced
- 2 cloves garlic, minced
- 1-inch piece ginger, minced
- 2 tbsp curry powder
- 1/2 cup coconut milk
- 1/2 cup tomato puree
- 1/2 cup chicken or vegetable broth
- Salt and pepper to taste
- Fresh cilantro for garnish

Step-by-Step Preparation:

1. Combine lamb, onion, garlic, and ginger in the slow cooker.
2. Stir in curry powder, coconut milk, tomato puree, and broth.
3. Season with salt and pepper.
4. Cook on low for 6 hours until lamb is tender.
5. Adjust seasoning to taste.
6. Garnish with fresh cilantro before serving.

Nutritional Facts: (Per serving)

- Calories: 580
- Protein: 35g
- Carbohydrates: 20g
- Fat: 40g
- Fiber: 4g
- Sodium: 500mg

With its depth of flavor and tender meat, this Lamb Curry is an ideal choice for those seeking a hearty, spice-infused meal that's both easy to prepare and deeply satisfying.

Recipe 07: Slow Cooker Thick and Chunky Beef Stew

Embrace the heartiness of a classic with this Slow Cooker Thick and Chunky Beef Stew. Specially portioned for one, it offers the perfect blend of tender beef and wholesome vegetables, simmered to perfection, ideal for a comforting, home-cooked meal.

Servings: 1

Prepping Time: 15 mins

Cook Time: 8 hrs

Difficulty: Easy

Ingredients:

- 200g beef chuck, cut into chunks
- 1 potato, cubed
- 1 carrot, sliced
- 1/2 onion, chopped
- 1 garlic clove, minced
- 1 cup beef broth
- 1 tbsp tomato paste
- 1/2 tsp each of thyme and rosemary
- Salt and pepper to taste

Step-by-Step Preparation:

1. Place beef, potato, carrot, onion, and garlic in the slow cooker.
2. Add beef broth and tomato paste.
3. Season with thyme, rosemary, salt, and pepper.
4. Cook on low for 8 hours until beef is tender and vegetables are soft.
5. Stir well and adjust seasoning as needed before serving.

Nutritional Facts: (Per serving)

- Calories: 520
- Protein: 38g
- Carbohydrates: 40g
- Fat: 22g
- Fiber: 6g
- Sodium: 700mg

This Slow Cooker Thick and Chunky Beef Stew is a testament to the joy of simple, hearty meals. It's perfect for those chilly evenings when you crave the warmth and comfort of a home-cooked stew.

Recipe 08: Home Made Stew and Dumplings

Immerse yourself in the comfort of a homemade stew and dumplings, a classic dish crafted in a slow cooker for a delightful single serving. This recipe combines tender meat with hearty vegetables and fluffy dumplings, embodying the essence of home-cooked warmth.

Servings: 1

Prepping Time: 20 mins

Cook Time: 7 hrs

Difficulty: Medium

Ingredients:

- 150g beef stew meat
- 1/2 potato, cubed
- 1 carrot, sliced
- 1/4 onion, chopped
- 1 cup beef broth
- 1/2 tsp mixed herbs
- Salt and pepper to taste
- For Dumplings:
  - 1/2 cup self-raising flour
  - 25g butter
  - 2 tbsp water

Step-by-Step Preparation:

1. Place beef, potato, carrot, and onion in the slow cooker.
2. Pour beef broth and season with mixed herbs, salt, and pepper.
3. Cook on low for 6 hours.
4. Mix flour and butter until crumbly for dumplings, then add water to form a dough.
5. Roll dough into small balls and place on top of the stew.
6. Cook for an additional hour until dumplings are cooked through.

Nutritional Facts: (Per serving)

- Calories: 650
- Protein: 40g
- Carbohydrates: 50g
- Fat: 30g
- Fiber: 5g
- Sodium: 800mg

This homemade stew and dumplings cooked in a slow cooker brings the nostalgic taste of comfort food right to your table. Perfect for a cozy night in, it's a hearty meal that promises to satisfy both hunger and soul.

Recipe 09: Cannellini Beans Beef Stew

Savor the rich blend of flavors in this Cannellini Beans Beef Stew, a slow cooker masterpiece perfect for a single serving. Combining tender beef with creamy cannellini beans, this dish is a hearty and satisfying meal, ideal for those seeking comfort in every spoonful.

Servings: 1

Prepping Time: 15 mins

Cook Time: 8 hrs

Difficulty: Easy

Ingredients:

- 150g beef stew meat
- 1/2 cup cannellini beans, soaked overnight
- 1 small carrot, diced
- 1/2 onion, chopped
- 1 garlic clove, minced
- 1 cup beef broth
- 1/2 tsp dried thyme
- Salt and pepper to taste

Step-by-Step Preparation:

1. Drain and rinse the soaked cannellini beans.
2. Place beef, beans, carrots, onion, and garlic in the slow cooker.
3. Pour in beef broth and season with thyme, salt, and pepper.
4. Cook on low for 8 hours until the beef is tender and the beans are cooked.
5. Adjust the seasoning as needed before serving.

Nutritional Facts: (Per serving)

- Calories: 550
- Protein: 35g
- Carbohydrates: 40g
- Fat: 25g
- Fiber: 10g
- Sodium: 700mg

Enjoy this Cannellini Beans Beef Stew from your slow cooker, a delightful, nutritious, and comforting meal. It's the perfect way to wind down after a long day, bringing a homemade touch to your dining experience.

Recipe 10: Baby Back Ribs

Indulge in Baby Back Ribs smoky, tender delight effortlessly cooked in a crockpot to create a barbecue sensation. This recipe serves up a single portion of fall-off-the-bone ribs smothered in a rich, tangy sauce, making it the perfect treat for those solo, cozy evenings.

Servings: 1

Prepping Time: 10 mins

Cook Time: 7 hrs

Difficulty: Easy

Ingredients:

- 4 baby back ribs
- 1/2 cup barbecue sauce
- 1 tbsp brown sugar
- 1 tbsp apple cider vinegar
- 1 tsp smoked paprika
- 1/2 tsp garlic powder
- Salt and pepper to taste

Step-by-Step Preparation:

1. Mix barbecue sauce, brown sugar, vinegar, smoked paprika, garlic powder, salt, and pepper.
2. Coat the ribs evenly with the sauce mixture.
3. Place the ribs in the crockpot, curving them around the pot if needed.
4. Cook on low for 7 hours until tender.
5. Optional: For a crispy exterior, broil ribs in the oven for 5 minutes after slow cooking.

Nutritional Facts: (Per serving)

- Calories: 800
- Protein: 40g
- Carbohydrates: 35g
- Fat: 55g
- Sugar: 25g
- Sodium: 950mg

These Crockpot Barbecue Baby Back Ribs are a simple yet satisfying way to enjoy a classic favorite. The slow cooker does all the work, leaving you with succulent ribs perfect for a relaxed and flavorful dining experience.

Chapter 02: Chicken for One

Recipe 11: Chicken Taco with Corn

Delight in the fusion of flavors with this Chicken Taco with Corn, a simple yet delicious slow cooker recipe perfect for a solo meal. Enjoy the tenderness of the chicken and the sweetness of corn, all wrapped up in a taco, making for a quick, flavorful, and satisfying meal.

Servings: 1

Prepping Time: 10 mins

Cook Time: 4 hrs

Difficulty: Easy

Ingredients:

- 1 chicken breast
- 1/2 cup corn kernels
- 1/2 tsp chili powder
- 1/4 tsp cumin
- 1/2 cup salsa
- Salt to taste
- 2 small tortillas
- Fresh cilantro for garnish
- Lime wedges for serving

Step-by-Step Preparation:

1. Place the chicken breast in the slow cooker.
2. Top with corn kernels, chili powder, cumin, and salsa.
3. Cook on low for 4 hours until the chicken is tender.
4. Shred the chicken and mix with the corn and cooking juices.
5. Warm the tortillas, then fill them with the chicken mixture.
6. Garnish with fresh cilantro and serve with lime wedges.

Nutritional Facts: (Per serving)

- Calories: 450
- Protein: 35g
- Carbohydrates: 45g
- Fat: 15g
- Fiber: 5g
- Sodium: 700mg

This Chicken Taco with Corn recipe is a delightful way to enjoy a classic favorite with a twist. It's perfect for when you crave something simple yet flavorful, offering a satisfying meal without the hassle.

Recipe 12: Shredded Chicken in Cream Cheese Sauce and Bacon

Experience the decadent combination of tender shredded chicken enveloped in a creamy cheese sauce, enhanced with the savory touch of bacon. This slow cooker recipe is perfectly portioned for one, offering a luxurious and comforting meal that's both effortless to prepare and delightful to savor.

Servings: 1

Prepping Time: 10 mins

Cook Time: 6 hrs

Difficulty: Easy

Ingredients:

- 1 chicken breast
- 1/4 cup cream cheese
- 2 slices of bacon, chopped
- 1/2 tsp garlic powder
- Salt and pepper to taste
- Chopped parsley for garnish

Step-by-Step Preparation:

1. Place the chicken breast in the slow cooker.
2. Season with garlic powder, salt, and pepper.
3. Spread cream cheese over the chicken.
4. Top with chopped bacon.
5. Cook on low for 6 hours until the chicken is tender.
6. Shred the chicken in the sauce and mix well.
7. Garnish with chopped parsley before serving.

Nutritional Facts: (Per serving)

- Calories: 480
- Protein: 38g
- Carbohydrates: 2g
- Fat: 35g
- Fiber: 0g
- Sodium: 820mg

Indulge in this Shredded Chicken in Cream Cheese Sauce and Bacon, a dish that combines simplicity with luxury. It's perfect for those evenings when you crave a rich, flavorful meal without the fuss of elaborate cooking.

Recipe 13: Crack Chicken Over Egg Pasta

Embark on a culinary journey with "Crack Chicken Over Egg Pasta," a slow cooker dish that perfectly combines creamy, flavorful chicken with the delicate texture of egg pasta. Ideal for a single serving, this recipe promises a mouth-watering experience that's both easy to prepare and deeply satisfying.

Servings: 1

Prepping Time: 15 mins

Cook Time: 6 hrs

Difficulty: Easy

Ingredients:

- 1 chicken breast
- 1/4 cup cream cheese
- 1 tbsp ranch seasoning
- 2 slices of bacon, cooked and crumbled
- 1/2 cup egg pasta
- Salt and pepper to taste
- Chopped chives for garnish

Step-by-Step Preparation:

1. Place the chicken breast in the slow cooker.
2. Top with cream cheese and ranch seasoning.
3. Cook on low for 6 hours until chicken is tender.
4. Boil egg pasta as per package instructions, then drain.
5. Mix the chicken in the cooker with the cream cheese sauce.
6. Serve the chicken over cooked egg pasta.
7. Garnish with crumbled bacon and chopped chives.

Nutritional Facts: (Per serving)

- Calories: 550
- Protein: 40g
- Carbohydrates: 35g
- Fat: 25g
- Fiber: 2g
- Sodium: 980mg

"Crack Chicken Over Egg Pasta" is an exquisite, effortless dish that brings a touch of gourmet to your everyday dining. Perfect for a solo treat, it's a comforting, creamy, and savory meal that will delight your taste buds.

Recipe 14: Chicken with Seasoning Mix

Savor the simplicity and flavor of this slow cooker chicken dish, perfectly seasoned and accompanied by creamer potatoes. It's a straightforward, one-serving recipe that effortlessly combines tender chicken with the comfort of flavorful potatoes, ideal for a satisfying and hassle-free meal.

Servings: 1

Prepping Time: 10 mins

Cook Time: 6 hrs

Difficulty: Easy

Ingredients:

- 1 chicken breast
- 1/2 tsp seasoning mix (e.g., Italian or Herbs de Provence)
- 1 cup creamer potatoes, halved
- Salt and pepper to taste
- 1/2 cup chicken broth

Step-by-Step Preparation:

1. Season the chicken breast with the seasoning mix, salt, and pepper.
2. Place the seasoned chicken and halved creamer potatoes in the slow cooker.
3. Pour chicken broth over the ingredients.
4. Cook on low for 6 hours until the chicken is tender and potatoes are cooked.
5. Adjust seasoning if needed before serving.

Nutritional Facts: (Per serving)

- Calories: 400
- Protein: 30g
- Carbohydrates: 40g
- Fat: 10g
- Fiber: 4g
- Sodium: 300mg

Enjoy this effortless yet delicious slow cooker chicken with seasoning mix and creamer potatoes, a meal that offers comfort and taste with minimal preparation. It's a delightful way to enjoy a wholesome, home-cooked meal, perfect for a cozy night in.

Recipe 15: Peanut Chicken

Dive into the exotic flavors of Peanut Chicken, a tantalizing slow cooker dish perfect for one. This recipe seamlessly blends the nutty richness of peanuts with tender chicken, creating a savory and slightly sweet delight that's easy to prepare and incredibly satisfying for a solo meal.

Servings: 1

Prepping Time: 15 mins

Cook Time: 4 hrs

Difficulty: Easy

Ingredients:

- 1 chicken breast
- 1/4 cup peanut butter
- 1 tbsp soy sauce
- 1 tsp honey
- 1/2 tsp garlic powder
- 1/4 tsp ginger powder
- 1/2 cup chicken broth
- Chopped peanuts and green onions for garnish

Step-by-Step Preparation:

1. Place chicken breast in the slow cooker.
2. Mix peanut butter, soy sauce, honey, garlic powder, and ginger powder in a bowl.
3. Pour the mixture over the chicken.
4. Add chicken broth to the slow cooker.
5. Cook on low for 4 hours until the chicken is tender.
6. Shred the chicken and mix it with the sauce.
7. Garnish with chopped peanuts and green onions.

Nutritional Facts: (Per serving)

- Calories: 480
- Protein: 38g
- Carbohydrates: 15g
- Fat: 30g
- Fiber: 2g
- Sodium: 800mg

Peanut Chicken in the slow cooker is a beautiful exploration of flavors, ideal for those seeking a unique and satisfying meal. It's a delightful blend of comfort and taste, ensuring a memorable dining experience.

Recipe 16: White Chili Chicken with Beans

Experience the comforting taste of White Chili Chicken with Beans and Corn, a slow cooker dish perfect for a nourishing single serving. This recipe combines the subtle flavors of white chicken chili with the heartiness of beans and the sweetness of corn, creating a deliciously balanced and satisfying meal.

Servings: 1

Prepping Time: 15 mins

Cook Time: 5 hrs

Difficulty: Easy

Ingredients:

- 1 chicken breast
- 1/2 cup cannellini beans, drained and rinsed
- 1/2 cup corn kernels
- 1/2 onion, chopped
- 1 garlic clove, minced
- 1 cup chicken broth
- 1/2 tsp cumin
- 1/4 tsp chili powder
- Salt and pepper to taste
- Fresh cilantro for garnish

Step-by-Step Preparation:

1. Place chicken breast, beans, corn, onion, and garlic in the slow cooker.
2. Pour chicken broth and season with cumin, chili powder, salt, and pepper.
3. Cook on low for 5 hours until chicken is tender.
4. Shred the chicken and mix it back into the stew.
5. Adjust seasoning if necessary and garnish with fresh cilantro before serving.

Nutritional Facts: (Per serving)

- Calories: 450
- Protein: 40g
- Carbohydrates: 40g
- Fat: 10g
- Fiber: 8g
- Sodium: 600mg

White Chili Chicken with Beans and Corn is a delightful slow cooker for a cozy, fuss-free meal. Its blend of flavors and textures makes it a wholesome and enjoyable dish, ideal for any day when you crave comfort food with a twist.

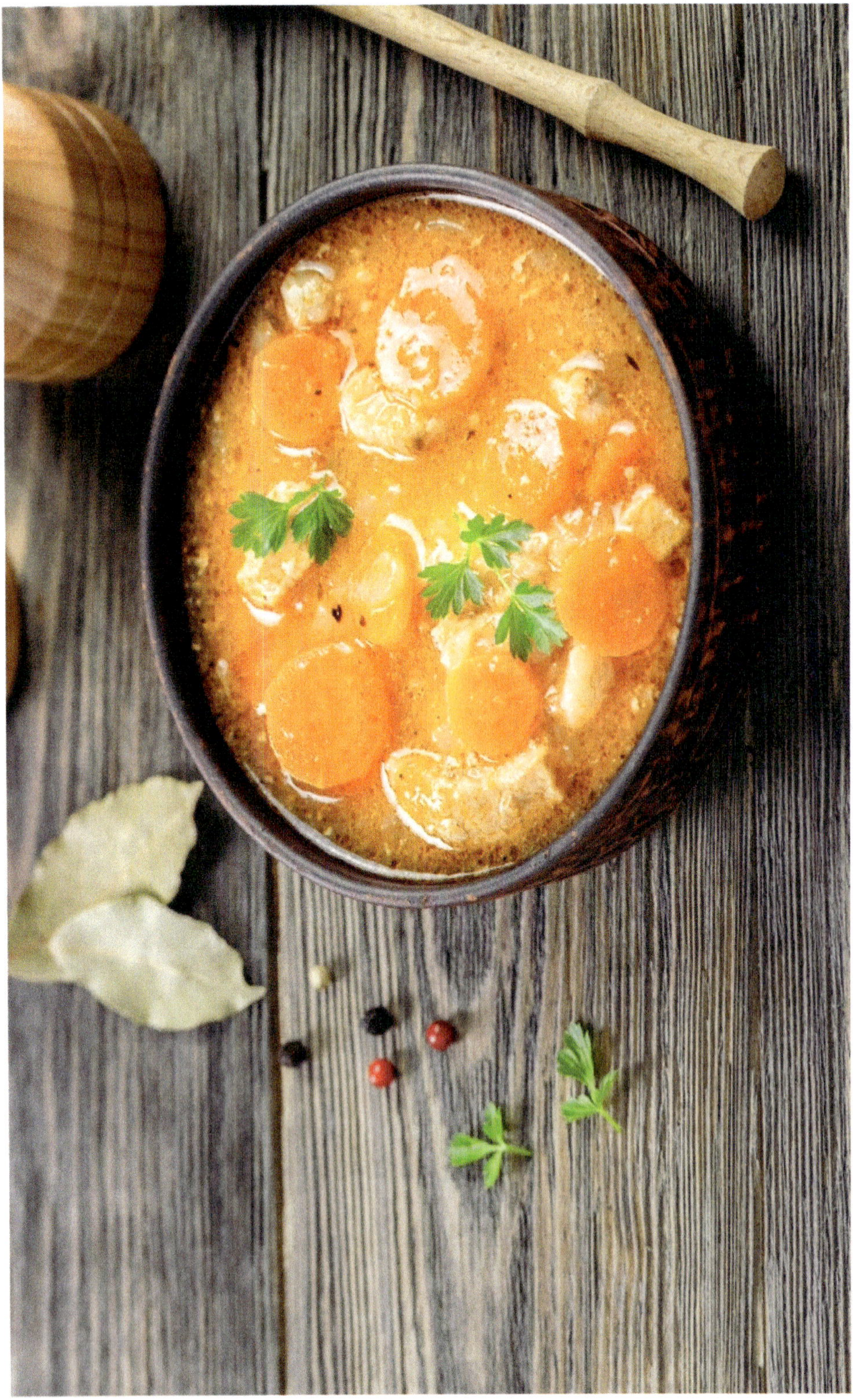

Recipe 17: Chicken Vegetable Stew

Savor the wholesome goodness of Chicken Vegetable Stew, a delightful slow cooker dish perfect for a solo meal. This comforting recipe blends tender chicken with a medley of fresh vegetables, creating a nourishing and flavorful stew that's easy to prepare and satisfying to enjoy.

Servings: 1

Prepping Time: 15 mins

Cook Time: 6 hrs

Difficulty: Easy

Ingredients:

- 1 chicken breast
- 1/2 cup diced carrots
- 1/2 cup chopped celery
- 1/2 onion, chopped
- 1 garlic clove, minced
- 1 cup chicken broth
- 1/2 tsp dried thyme
- Salt and pepper to taste

Step-by-Step Preparation:

1. Place chicken breast in the slow cooker.
2. Add diced carrots, chopped celery, onion, and minced garlic.
3. Pour in chicken broth and season with thyme, salt, and pepper.
4. Cook on low for 6 hours until chicken is tender and vegetables are soft.
5. Shred the chicken and stir it back into the stew.
6. Adjust seasoning if needed before serving.

Nutritional Facts: (Per serving)

- Calories: 300
- Protein: 30g
- Carbohydrates: 20g
- Fat: 10g
- Fiber: 4g
- Sodium: 500mg

This Chicken Vegetable Stew is a heartwarming dish that combines simple ingredients and slow cooking. It's ideal for those evenings when you crave a homemade meal that's both healthful and gratifying.

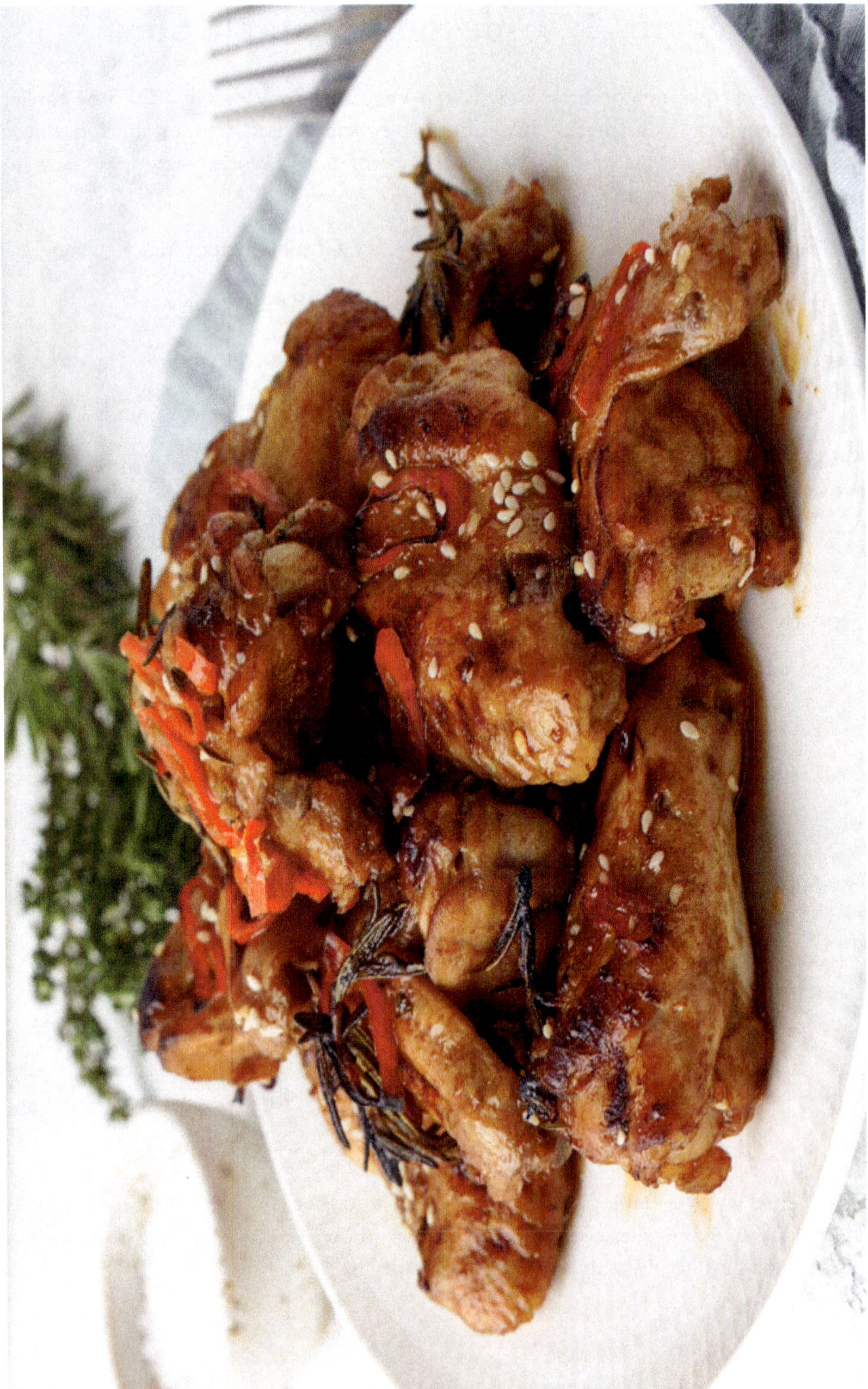

Recipe 18: Barbecue Chicken Wings

Indulge in the tantalizing flavors of Barbecue Chicken Wings, a perfect blend of sweet and spicy, slow-cooked to perfection and finished in the oven. This recipe delivers a solo serving of succulent wings coated in a rich BBQ sauce, offering a finger-licking good experience that's easy to prepare and irresistibly delicious.

Servings: 1

Prepping Time: 15 mins

Cook Time: 4 hrs

Difficulty: Medium

Ingredients:

- 6 chicken wings
- 1/2 cup barbecue sauce
- 1 tbsp honey
- 1 tsp hot sauce
- 1/2 tsp garlic powder
- 1/2 tsp smoked paprika
- Salt and pepper to taste

Step-by-Step Preparation:

1. Mix barbecue sauce, honey, hot sauce, garlic powder, smoked paprika, salt, and pepper in a bowl.
2. Coat chicken wings evenly with the sauce mixture.
3. Place wings in the slow cooker.
4. Cook on low for 4 hours until tender.
5. Preheat oven to 400°F (200°C).
6. Transfer wings to a baking sheet and bake for 10 minutes for a crispy finish.
7. Serve the wings coated in the remaining BBQ sauce.

Nutritional Facts: (Per serving)

- Calories: 550
- Protein: 35g
- Carbohydrates: 40g
- Fat: 25g
- Sugar: 20g
- Sodium: 800mg

These sweet and spicy Barbecue Chicken Wings slow-cooked and oven-finished, are a delightful treat that combines ease of preparation with gourmet flavors. Perfect for a solo indulgence, they promise a mouthwatering experience that satisfies your BBQ cravings.

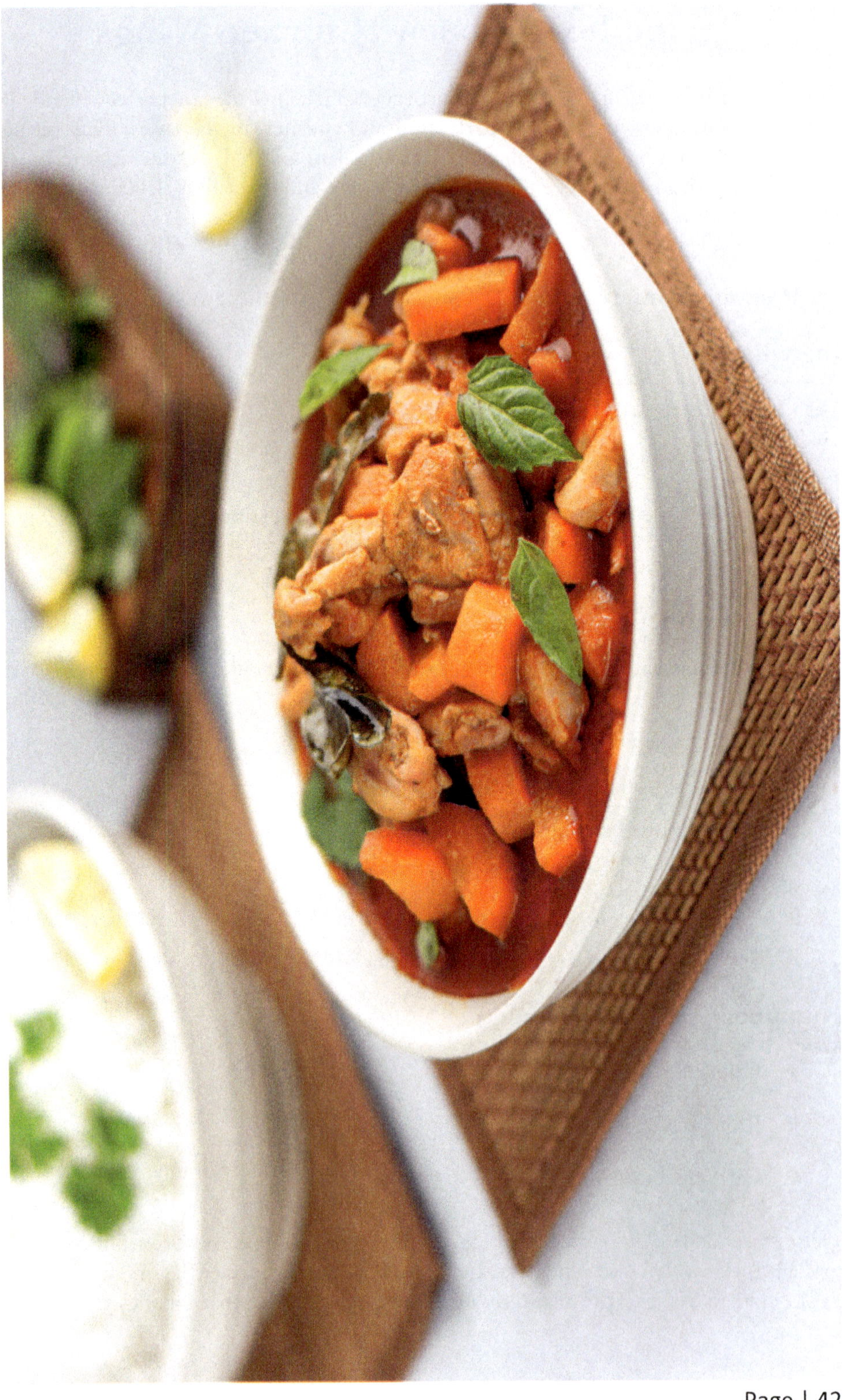

Recipe 19: Thai Red Chicken Curry

Immerse yourself in the vibrant and aromatic world of Thai cuisine with this Thai Red Chicken Curry, a dish that beautifully melds the heat of red curry with the freshness of basil leaves. Served with rice and a squeeze of lemon, this slow cooker recipe offers a perfect single serving for a flavorful and exotic meal.

Servings: 1

Prepping Time: 15 mins

Cook Time: 4 hrs

Difficulty: Medium

Ingredients:

- 1 chicken breast, diced
- 2 tbsp Thai red curry paste
- 1/2 cup coconut milk
- 1/2 red bell pepper, sliced
- 1/4 onion, sliced
- 1/2 cup bamboo shoots
- 1 tbsp fish sauce
- 1 tsp sugar
- Fresh basil leaves
- 1/2 cup cooked rice
- Lemon wedge for serving

Step-by-Step Preparation:

1. Place diced chicken in the slow cooker.
2. Add red curry paste, coconut milk, bell pepper, onion, and bamboo shoots.
3. Stir in fish sauce and sugar.
4. Cook on low for 4 hours until chicken is tender.
5. Serve over cooked rice garnished with fresh basil leaves.
6. Squeeze lemon over the curry before enjoying it.

Nutritional Facts: (Per serving)

- Calories: 550
- Protein: 35g
- Carbohydrates: 45g
- Fat: 25g
- Fiber: 3g
- Sodium: 800mg

This Thai Red Chicken Curry served with rice, and a hint of lemon brings a piece of Thailand to your table. It's an exquisite, easy-to-make dish that provides a perfect escape into a world of flavors, ideal for a special yet effortless dining experience.

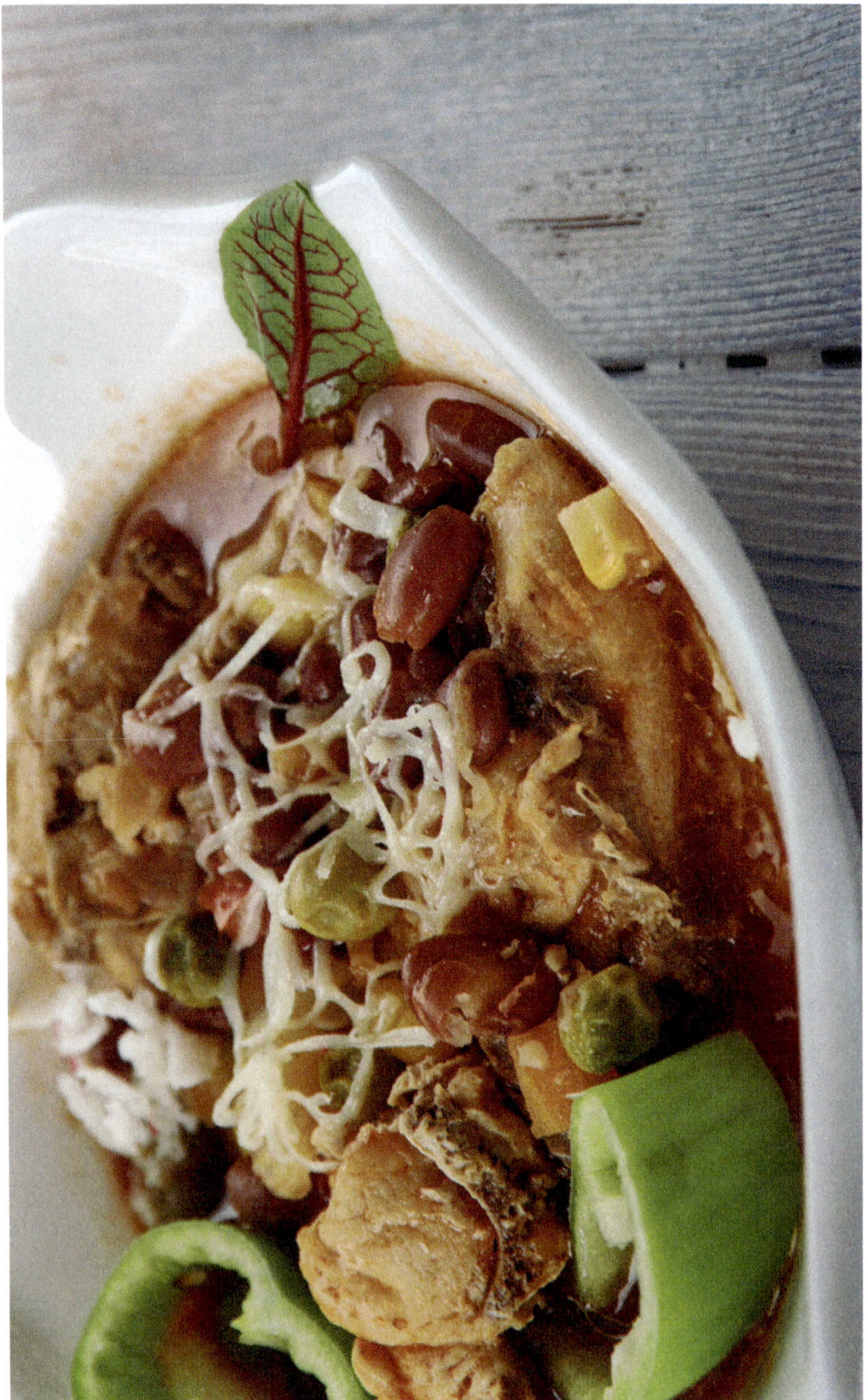

Recipe 20: Tex-Mex Chicken Stew

Savor the rich, spicy flavors of Tex-Mex cuisine with this comforting slow-cooker chicken stew. Perfect for a cozy night in, this hearty dish brings a fusion of bold Texan and Mexican tastes to your table with minimal effort.

Servings: 1

Prepping Time: 15 minutes

Cook Time: 6 hours

Difficulty: Easy

Ingredients:

- 1 chicken breast, boneless and skinless
- 1/2 cup diced tomatoes
- 1/4 cup black beans, drained
- 1/4 cup corn kernels
- 1/2 small onion, chopped
- 1 garlic clove, minced
- 1/2 teaspoon ground cumin
- 1/4 teaspoon chili powder
- 1/4 teaspoon paprika
- 1 cup chicken broth
- Salt and pepper, to taste
- Fresh cilantro for garnish

Step-by-Step Preparation:

1. Place the chicken breast at the bottom of the slow cooker.
2. Add diced tomatoes, black beans, corn, onion, and garlic.
3. Sprinkle cumin, chili powder, paprika, salt, and pepper over the ingredients.
4. Pour chicken broth into the slow cooker, ensuring the ingredients are well-covered.
5. Cover and cook on low for 6 hours.
6. Once cooked, shred the chicken inside the cooker using two forks.
7. Stir well to mix everything.
8. Garnish with fresh cilantro before serving.

Nutritional Facts: (Per serving)

- Calories: 350
- Protein: 28g
- Carbohydrates: 40g
- Fat: 8g
- Sodium: 800mg
- Fiber: 7g

End your day with this delightful Tex-Mex Chicken Stew, a perfect single-serving comfort meal. Its blend of spices and tender chicken makes for an effortless yet flavorful dining experience, proving that good things come in small, delicious packages.

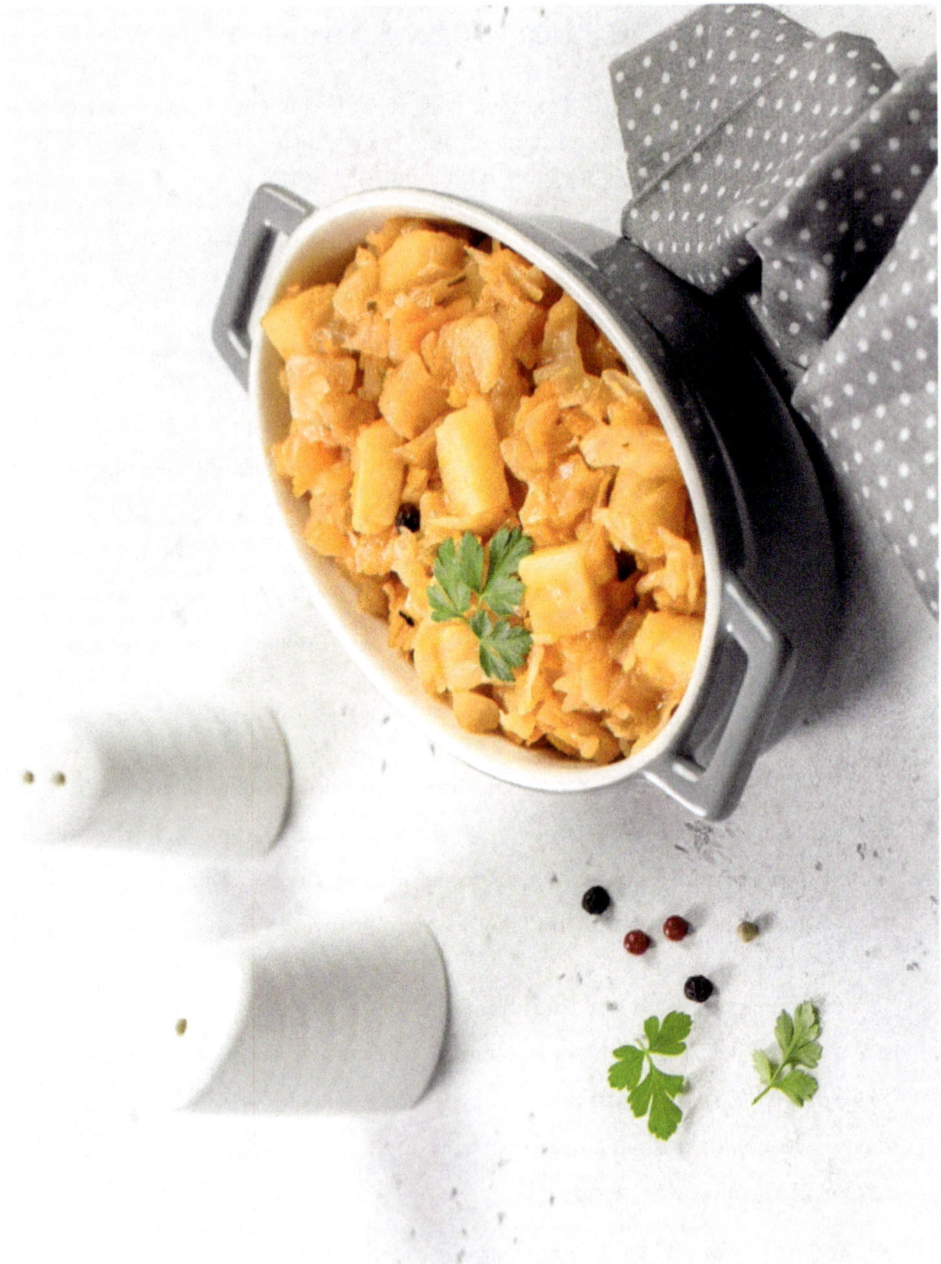

Chapter 03: Vegetarian Delights

Recipe 21: Stewed Cabbage Potato

Delight in the homely comforts of this Stewed Cabbage Potato dish, a vegetarian recipe made easy with your slow cooker. Packed with the wholesome goodness of vegetables, it's perfect for a nourishing meal any day of the week.

Servings: 1

Prepping Time: 10 minutes

Cook Time: 4 hours

Difficulty: Easy

Ingredients:

- 1 cup chopped cabbage
- 1 medium potato, diced
- 1/2 carrot, sliced
- 1/4 onion, chopped
- 1 garlic clove, minced
- 1/2 teaspoon dried thyme
- 1/2 teaspoon paprika
- 1 cup vegetable broth
- Salt and pepper, to taste

Step-by-Step Preparation:

1. Place the chopped cabbage, diced potato, sliced carrot, and chopped onion into the slow cooker.
2. Add minced garlic, dried thyme, and paprika.
3. Pour the vegetable broth over the vegetables, ensuring they are well-covered.
4. Season with salt and pepper to taste.
5. Cover and cook on low for 4 hours until the vegetables are tender.
6. Stir gently before serving to blend the flavors.

Nutritional Facts: (Per serving)

- Calories: 180
- Protein: 4g
- Carbohydrates: 40g
- Fat: 0.5g
- Sodium: 480mg
- Fiber: 6g

Conclude your day with this simple yet satisfying Stewed Cabbage Potato dish, a testament to the flavorful possibilities of vegetarian cooking. It's a fuss-free, one-pot wonder that brings warmth and nutrition to your table with every spoonful.

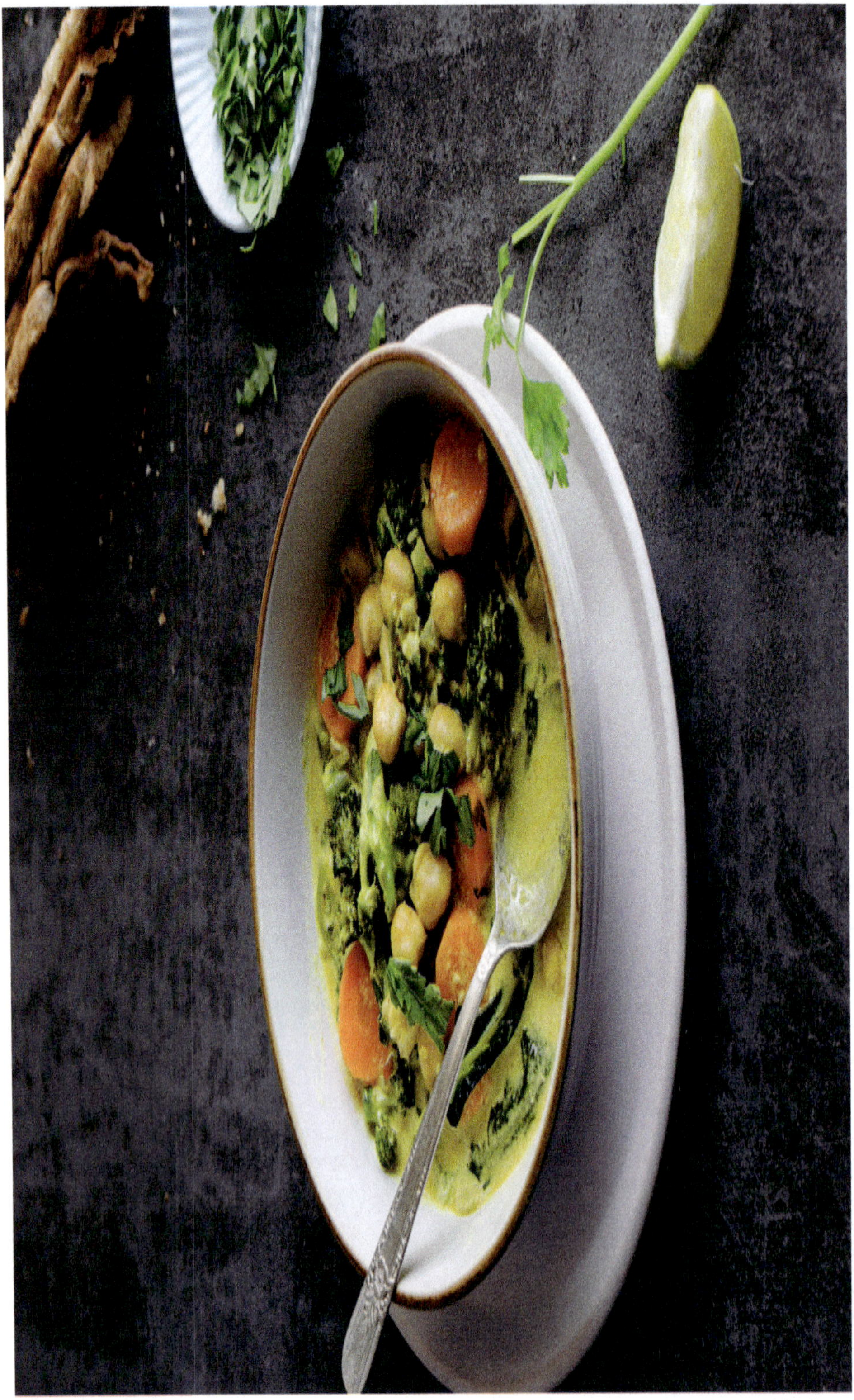

Recipe 22: Chickpea, Broccoli, Carrot Curry Cooked in Coconut Milk

Indulge in the creamy and aromatic delight of a vegetarian chickpea, broccoli, and carrot curry simmered in coconut milk. This easy-to-make dish, paired with a slice of warm bread toast, is a perfect symphony of flavors and textures for a satisfying solo meal.

Servings: 1

Prepping Time: 10 minutes

Cook Time: 6 hours

Difficulty: Easy

Ingredients:

- 1/2 cup chickpeas, soaked overnight
- 1/2 cup broccoli florets
- 1/2 carrot, chopped
- 1/4 onion, diced
- 1 garlic clove, minced
- 1 teaspoon curry powder
- 1/2 cup coconut milk
- Salt and pepper, to taste
- 1 slice whole grain bread

Step-by-Step Preparation:

1. Drain and rinse the soaked chickpeas, adding them to the slow cooker.
2. Add broccoli florets, chopped carrot, diced onion, and minced garlic.
3. Sprinkle in curry powder, salt, and pepper.
4. Pour coconut milk over the mixture, ensuring even coverage.
5. Cover and cook on low for 6 hours, until vegetables are tender and flavors meld.
6. Toast the whole-grain bread to your liking.
7. Serve the curry alongside the toasted bread.

Nutritional Facts: (Per serving)

- Calories: 325
- Protein: 11g
- Carbohydrates: 45g
- Fat: 13g
- Fiber: 9g
- Sodium: 300mg

Enjoy this simple yet delicious vegetarian chickpea, broccoli, and carrot curry, a dish that brings the warmth of home-cooked meals into your kitchen. Perfect for any day, it's a testament to how slow-cooked flavors and wholesome ingredients can elevate a single-serving meal into a culinary delight.

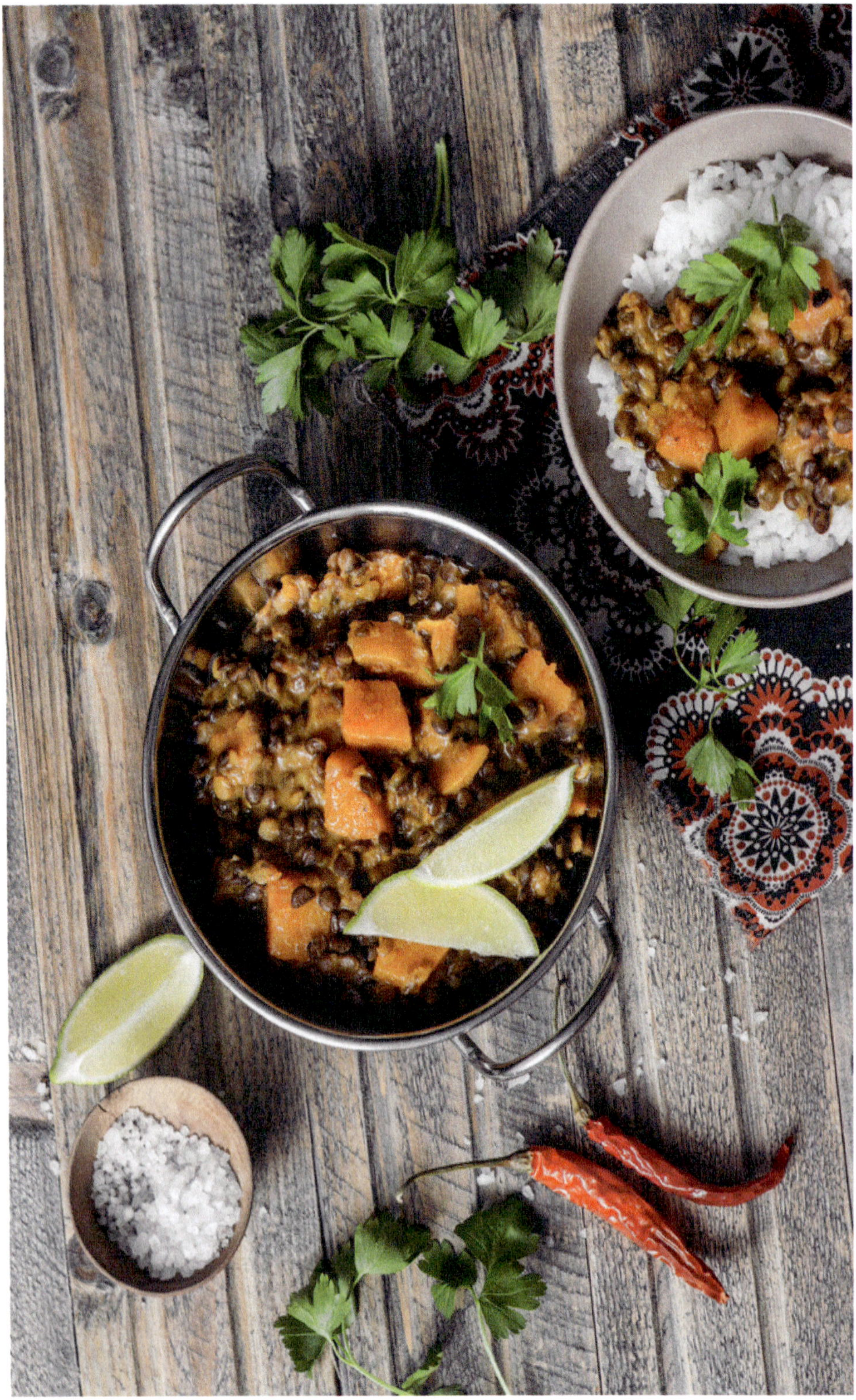

Recipe 23: Pumpkin Lentil Curry and Rice

Immerse yourself in the rich and comforting flavors of Pumpkin Lentil Curry and Rice, a vegetarian feast that's as nourishing as it is delicious. This slow cooker recipe is a breeze, offering a delightful blend of spices, pumpkin, and lentils, all served over fluffy rice.

Servings: 1

Prepping Time: 15 minutes

Cook Time: 5 hours

Difficulty: Easy

Ingredients:

- 1/2 cup diced pumpkin
- 1/4 cup red lentils
- 1/2 cup canned tomatoes, chopped
- 1/4 onion, chopped
- 1 garlic clove, minced
- 1/2 teaspoon curry powder
- 1/4 teaspoon cumin
- 1 cup vegetable broth
- 1/2 cup cooked rice
- Salt and pepper, to taste

Step-by-Step Preparation:

1. Place diced pumpkin, red lentils, chopped tomatoes, onion, and minced garlic in the slow cooker.
2. Sprinkle in curry powder and cumin.
3. Pour vegetable broth over the mixture. Season with salt and pepper.
4. Cover and cook on low for 5 hours, until lentils and pumpkin are tender.
5. Prepare rice according to package instructions.
6. Serve the curry over the cooked rice, ensuring a hearty mix of ingredients in each serving.

Nutritional Facts: (Per serving)

- Calories: 380
- Protein: 15g
- Carbohydrates: 75g
- Fat: 2g
- Fiber: 15g
- Sodium: 300mg

Wrap up your day with this Pumpkin Lentil Curry and Rice, a dish that satisfies your hunger and brings a sense of culinary adventure to your dining table. It's a testament to the power of simple ingredients, slow-cooked to perfection, to create a wholesome and heartwarming meal.

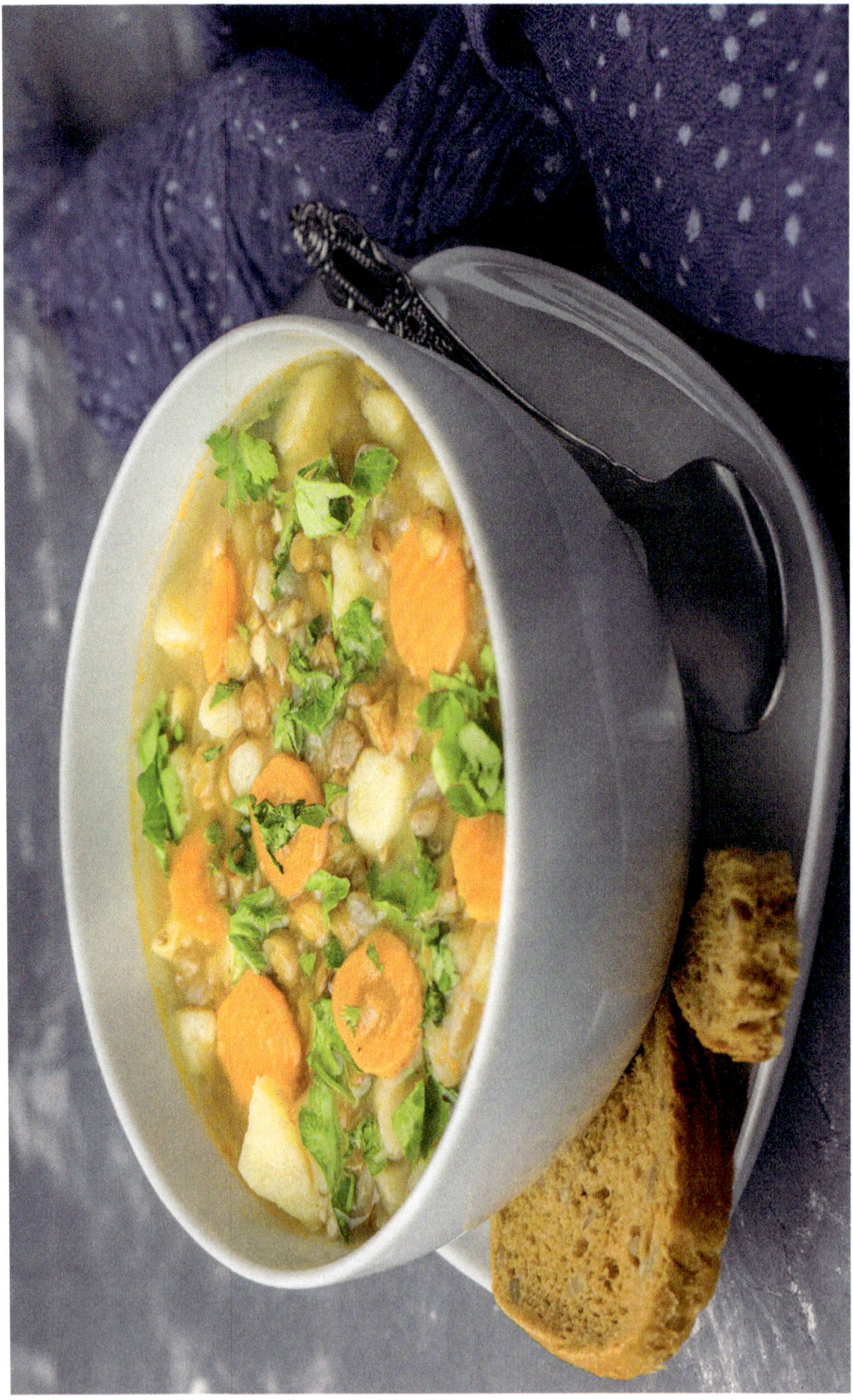

Recipe 24: Vegan Lentil Soup

Dive into the wholesome goodness of Vegan Lentil Soup, a perfect blend of nutrition and flavor. This slow cooker recipe makes preparing a hearty, comforting soup effortless. Ideal for busy days or when you crave a simple yet satisfying vegetarian meal just for yourself.

Servings: 1

Prepping Time: 10 minutes

Cook Time: 6 hours

Difficulty: Easy

Ingredients:

- 1/2 cup brown lentils
- 1/4 cup chopped carrots
- 1/4 cup chopped celery
- 1/4 onion, diced
- 1 garlic clove, minced
- 1/2 teaspoon dried thyme
- 1/4 teaspoon ground cumin
- 2 cups vegetable broth
- Salt and pepper, to taste

Step-by-Step Preparation:

1. Add brown lentils, chopped carrots, celery, and diced onion to the slow cooker.
2. Include minced garlic, dried thyme, and ground cumin.
3. Pour in vegetable broth and season with salt and pepper.
4. Cover and cook on low for 6 hours, until lentils are tender and flavors are well-blended.
5. Stir the soup before serving, adjusting seasoning if necessary.

Nutritional Facts: (Per serving)

- Calories: 260
- Protein: 18g
- Carbohydrates: 45g
- Fat: 1g
- Fiber: 15g
- Sodium: 480mg

Relish this Vegan Lentil Soup, a dish that brings comfort and nourishment to your table. It's a testament to the simplicity and heartiness of plant-based ingredients, creating a meal that's good for you and full of rich, savory flavors.

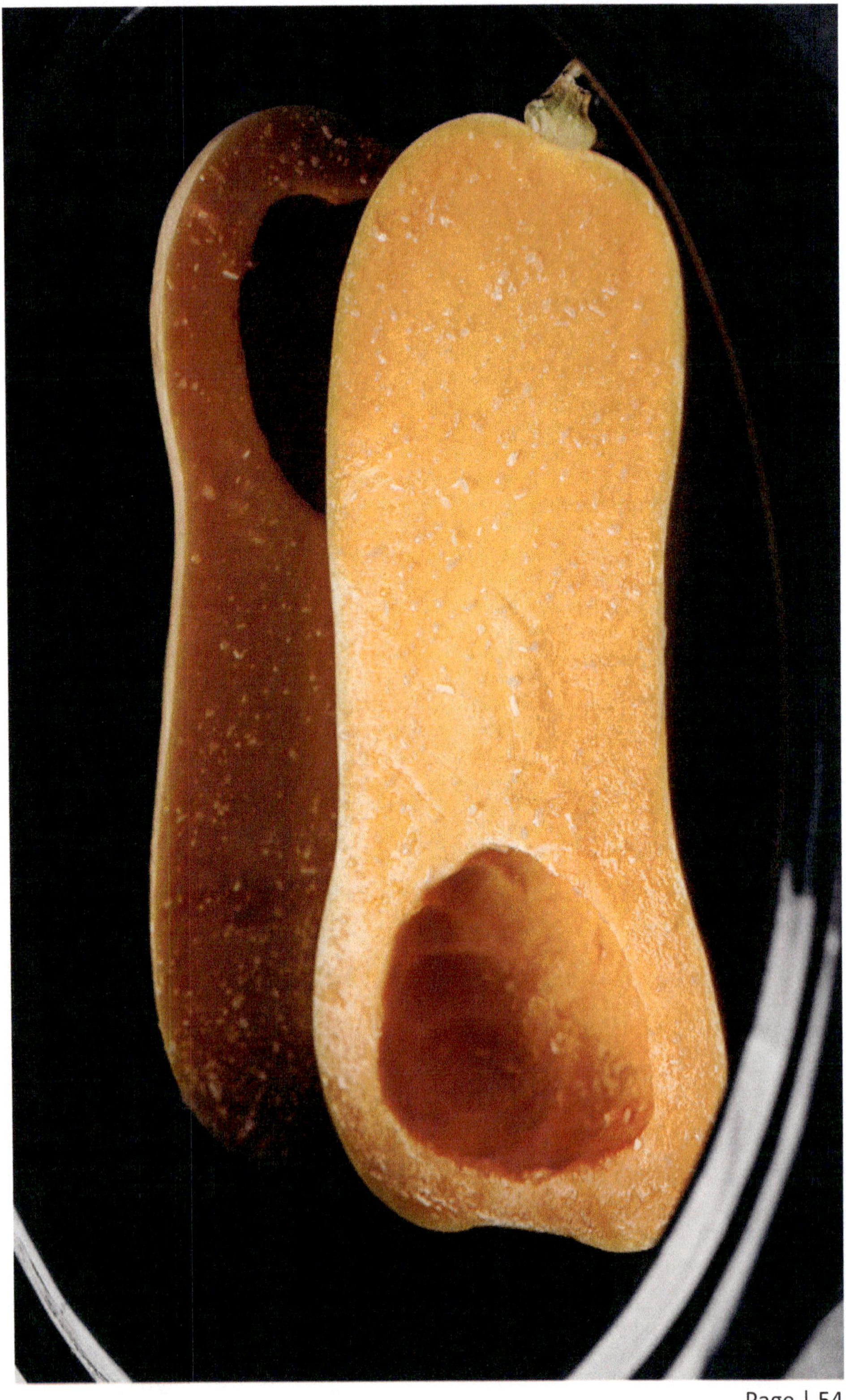

Recipe 25: Butternut Squash

Indulge in the comforting flavors of this Slow Cooker Vegetarian Butternut Squash dish. Perfect for a cozy meal, this recipe showcases the natural sweetness and creaminess of butternut squash, effortlessly prepared in a slow cooker.

Servings: 1

Prepping Time: 10 minutes

Cook Time: 4 hours

Difficulty: Easy

Ingredients:

- 1 medium butternut squash, halved and seeded
- 1 tbsp olive oil
- ½ tsp salt
- ¼ tsp black pepper
- 1 tsp honey or maple syrup (optional)
- ½ tsp ground cinnamon
- ¼ tsp ground nutmeg

Step-by-Step Preparation:

1. Brush the inside of each squash half with olive oil. Season with salt, pepper, cinnamon, and nutmeg.
2. Place the squash halves in the slow cooker and cut side up.
3. Drizzle honey or maple syrup over the squash for added sweetness.
4. Cover and cook on low for 3-4 hours or until the squash is tender.
5. Once cooked, let it cool slightly before serving.

Nutritional Facts: (Per serving)

- Calories: 180
- Carbohydrates: 31g
- Protein: 2g
- Fat: 7g
- Fiber: 5g
- Sugar: 6g

Enjoy this simple yet delicious butternut squash recipe, a perfect solo meal that brings warmth and nutrition to your table. Its easy preparation makes it a favorite for busy evenings or relaxed weekends.

Page | 56

Recipe 26: Vegetable Ratatouille

Savor the essence of French cuisine with this delightful Vegetable Ratatouille, a slow-cooker vegetarian recipe ideal for a nourishing solo meal. This dish brings together a melody of fresh vegetables, simmered to perfection, offering a taste of Provence in every bite.

Servings: 1

Prepping Time: 15 minutes

Cook Time: 6 hours

Difficulty: Easy

Ingredients:

- 1 small zucchini, sliced
- 1 small yellow squash, sliced
- ½ bell pepper, chopped
- 1 small eggplant, cubed
- 1 medium tomato, diced
- 1 garlic clove, minced
- 2 tbsp olive oil
- ½ tsp dried basil
- ½ tsp dried oregano
- Salt and pepper to taste

Step-by-Step Preparation:

1. Layer the zucchini, yellow squash, bell pepper, eggplant, and tomato in the slow cooker.
2. Sprinkle minced garlic, basil, oregano, salt, and pepper over the vegetables.
3. Drizzle with olive oil.
4. Cover and cook on low for 6 hours, stirring occasionally.
5. Once cooked, adjust seasoning if necessary and serve warm.

Nutritional Facts: (Per serving)

- Calories: 250
- Carbohydrates: 35g
- Protein: 6g
- Fat: 12g
- Fiber: 10g
- Sugar: 20g

This Vegetable Ratatouille is more than just a meal; it celebrates fresh, wholesome ingredients simmered to bring out their best flavors. Enjoy this comforting dish that's as nourishing as it is satisfying, perfect for a tranquil evening at home.

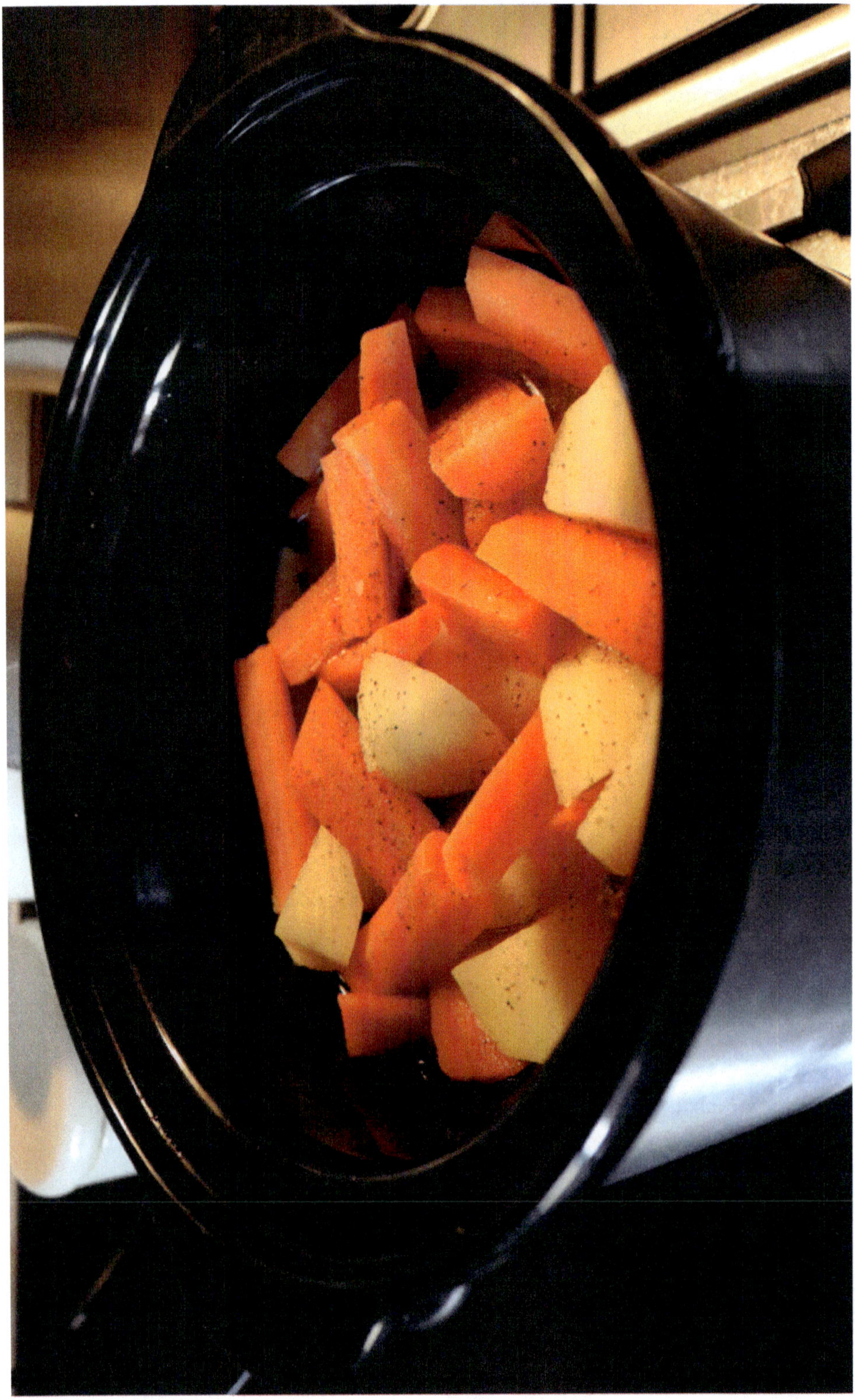

Recipe 27: Carrot Potatoes Green Beans

Embark on a flavorful journey with this Vegan Slow Cooker dish, featuring a hearty blend of carrots, potatoes, and green beans. This recipe is a testament to the simplicity and richness of plant-based ingredients, creating a comforting and nutritious meal perfect for any day.

Servings: 1

Prepping Time: 15 minutes

Cook Time: 4 hours

Difficulty: Easy

Ingredients:

- 2 medium carrots, sliced
- 1 large potato, cubed
- 1 cup green beans, trimmed
- 1 small onion, chopped
- 2 cloves garlic, minced
- ¾ cup vegetable broth
- ½ tsp dried thyme
- ¼ tsp ground black pepper
- Salt to taste

Step-by-Step Preparation:

1. Place the carrots, potatoes, and green beans in the slow cooker.
2. Add the chopped onion and minced garlic.
3. Pour the vegetable broth over the vegetables.
4. Season with thyme, black pepper, and salt.
5. Cover and cook on low for 4 hours until vegetables are tender.
6. Stir gently before serving.

Nutritional Facts: (Per serving)

- Calories: 320
- Carbohydrates: 72g
- Protein: 8g
- Fat: 1g
- Fiber: 14g
- Sugar: 12g

Relish in the simplicity and wholesomeness of this Vegan Vegetable Medley. It's a perfect example of how a few essential ingredients, slow-cooked to perfection, can transform into a delectable and satisfying meal that nourishes both body and soul.

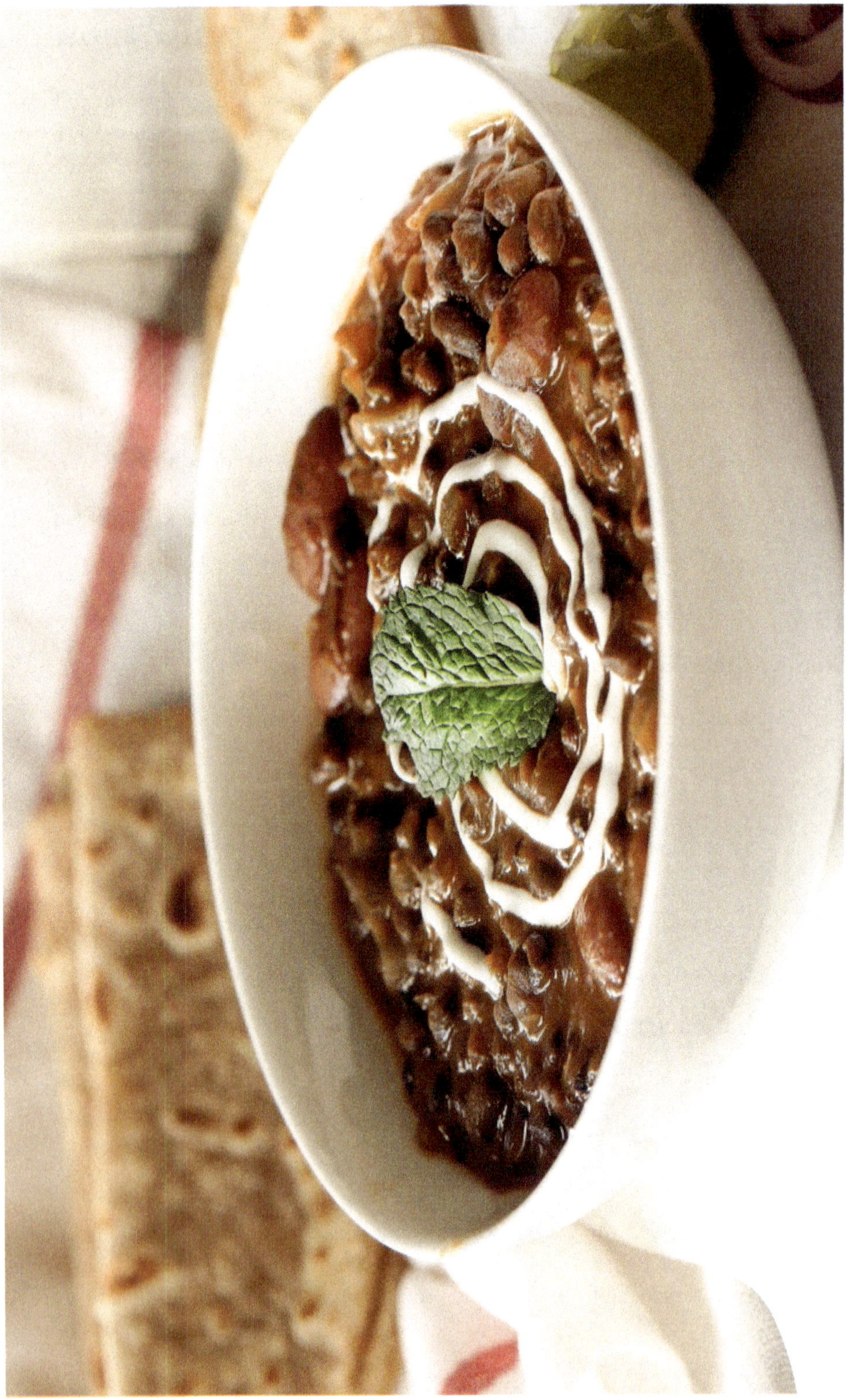

Recipe 28: Dal Makhani

Discover the rich flavors of Indian cuisine with this comforting Dal Makhani, a classic black lentil curry perfectly paired with Paratha or Roti. Prepared in a slow cooker, this vegetarian dish is a symphony of spices and textures, offering one a wholesome and satisfying meal.

Servings: 1

Prepping Time: 20 minutes

Cook Time: 8 hours

Difficulty: Medium

Ingredients:

- ½ cup black lentils, soaked overnight
- 1 large tomato, pureed
- 1 small onion, finely chopped
- 2 cloves garlic, minced
- 1-inch piece ginger, grated
- 2 tbsp cream or coconut milk
- 1 tsp cumin seeds
- ½ tsp gram masala
- ¼ tsp turmeric powder
- ¼ tsp red chili powder
- Salt to taste
- 2 tsp butter or oil
- 1 Paratha or Roti, for serving

Step-by-Step Preparation:

1. Rinse and drain the soaked lentils.
2. Combine lentils, tomato puree, onion, garlic, and ginger in the slow cooker.
3. Add cumin seeds, gram masala, turmeric, chili powder, and salt.
4. Pour in enough water to cover the lentils.
5. Cook on low for 8 hours until lentils are tender.
6. Stir in cream or coconut milk, and cook for another 30 minutes.
7. Heat butter or oil in a pan and pour over the dal to temper.
8. Serve hot with a Paratha or Roti.

Nutritional Facts: (Per serving, excluding Paratha/Roti)

- Calories: 360
- Carbohydrates: 54g
- Protein: 25g
- Fat: 9g
- Fiber: 15g
- Sugar: 4g

Enjoy the comfort and flavors of this Dal Makhani, a dish embodying the heart of Indian home cooking. Whether enjoyed as a hearty dinner or a special meal, it's a fulfilling and flavorful escape into culinary delight.

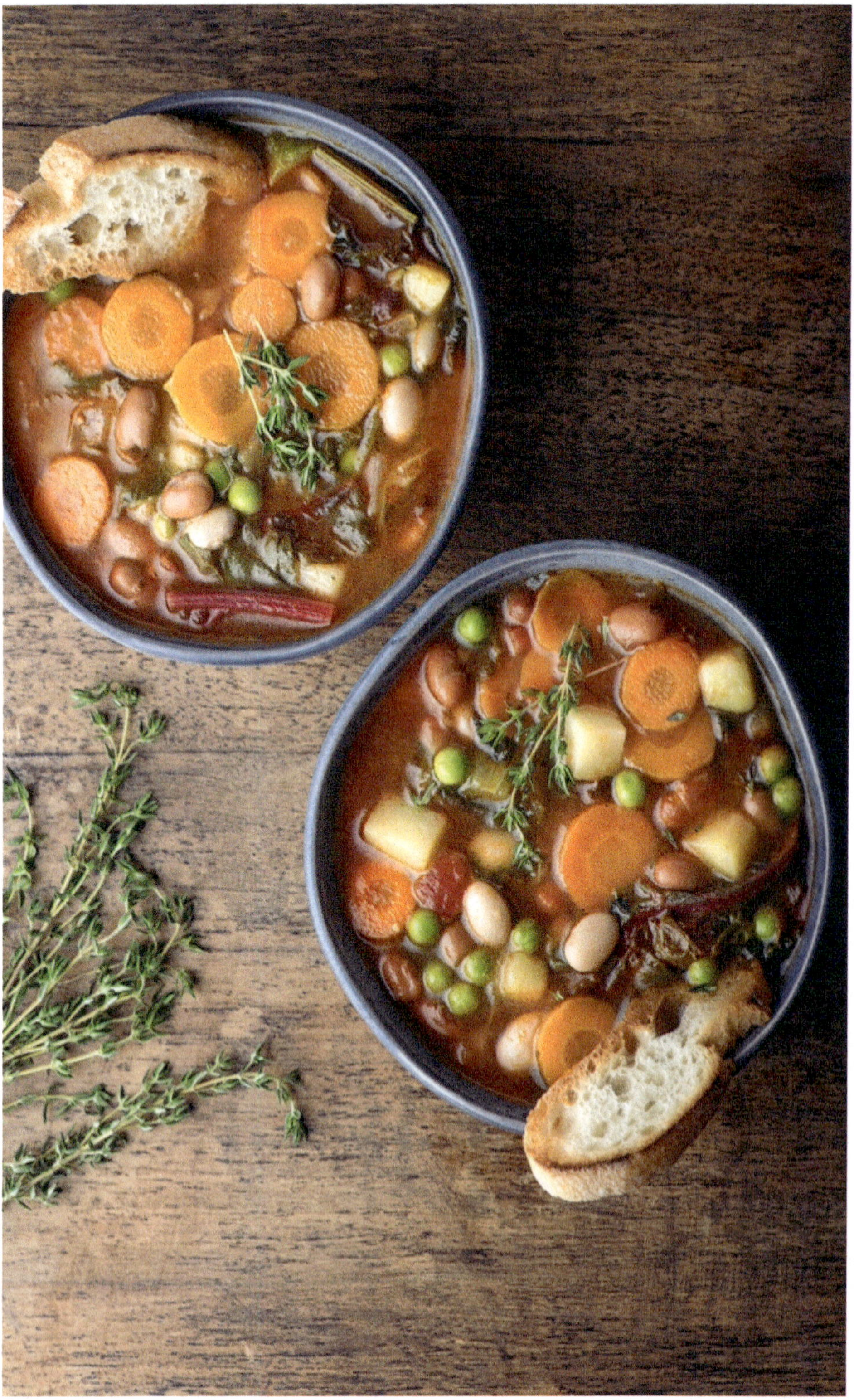

Recipe 29: Minestrone Vegetable Soup

Experience the comforting embrace of Italian cuisine with this Minestrone Vegetable Soup, a slow cooker recipe combining fresh vegetables and herbs. Topped with pieces of toasted bread, this soup is a warm, nourishing meal perfect for any day, embodying the simplicity and heartiness of traditional Italian cooking.

Servings: 1

Prepping Time: 15 minutes

Cook Time: 6 hours

Difficulty: Easy

Ingredients:

- ½ cup diced carrots
- ½ cup diced celery
- ½ cup chopped tomatoes
- ¼ cup chopped onion
- ¼ cup canned kidney beans rinsed and drained
- 1 garlic clove, minced
- 2 cups vegetable broth
- 1 bay leaf
- ½ tsp dried oregano
- ½ tsp dried basil
- Salt and pepper to taste
- 1 slice of bread, toasted and cubed
- Fresh parsley for garnish

Step-by-Step Preparation:

1. Add carrots, celery, tomatoes, onion, kidney beans, and garlic to the slow cooker.
2. Pour in the vegetable broth.
3. Add the bay leaf, oregano, basil, salt, and pepper.
4. Cover and cook on low for 6 hours.
5. Remove the bay leaf.
6. Serve hot soup, topped with toasted bread cubes and garnished with fresh parsley.

Nutritional Facts: (Per serving)

- Calories: 230
- Carbohydrates: 44g
- Protein: 10g
- Fat: 2g
- Fiber: 10g
- Sugar: 9g

This Minestrone Vegetable Soup, topped with crunchy toasted bread, is not just a meal but a celebration of hearty, wholesome flavors. It's the perfect way to indulge in the comforting joys of Italian cooking, conveniently prepared in your slow cooker.

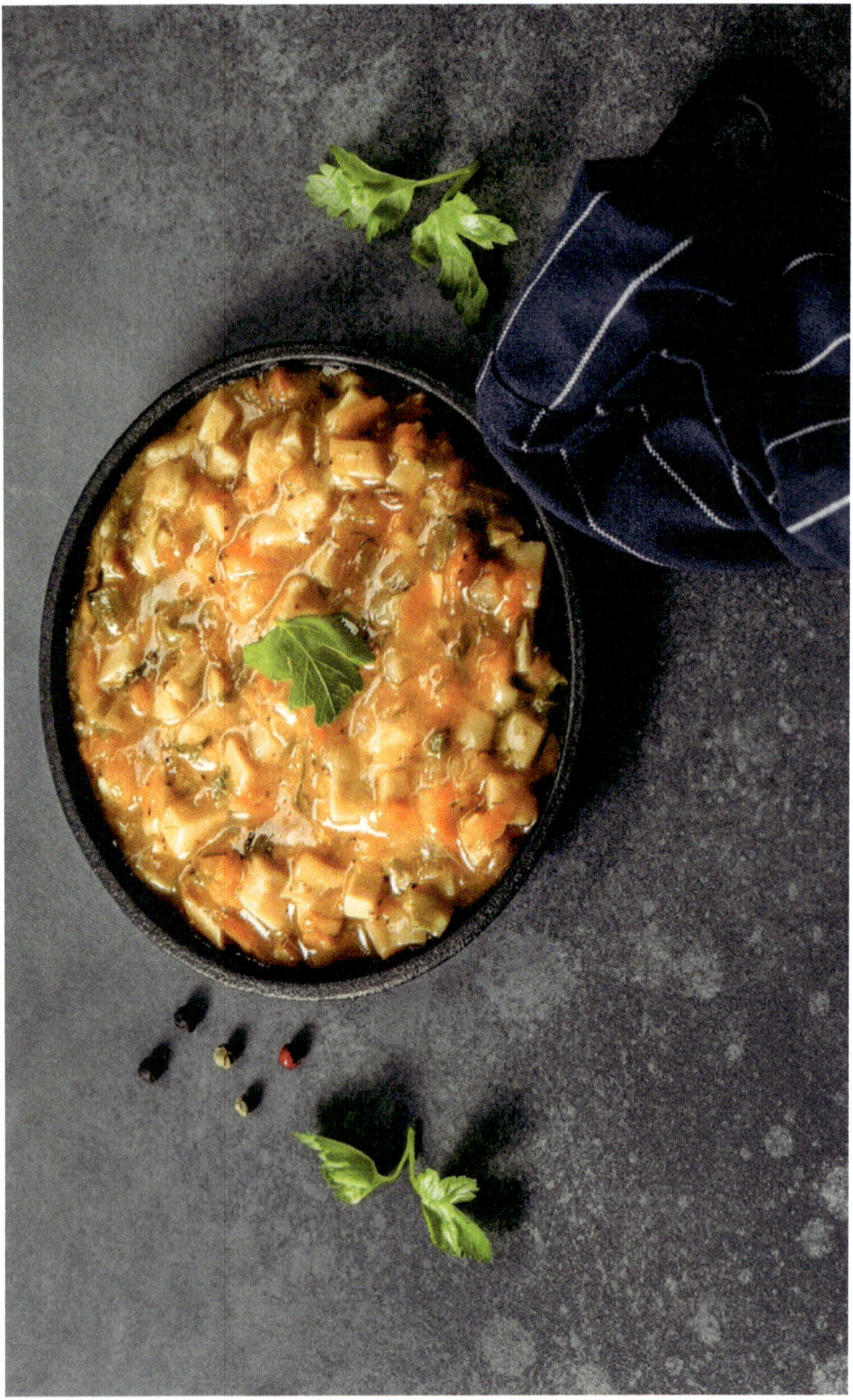

Recipe 30: Mushroom Vegan Lentil Stew

Immerse yourself in the earthy flavors of this Mushroom Vegan Lentil Stew, a hearty and nutritious slow cooker dish. Perfect for those seeking a wholesome and satisfying meal, this stew combines the umami richness of mushrooms with the heartiness of lentils, creating a comforting dish that's both flavorful and easy to prepare.

Servings: 1

Prepping Time: 15 minutes

Cook Time: 6 hours

Difficulty: Easy

Ingredients:

- ½ cup green lentils, rinsed
- 1 cup mushrooms, sliced
- 1 small onion, diced
- 1 clove garlic, minced
- 2 cups vegetable broth
- ½ tsp dried thyme
- ½ tsp dried rosemary
- Salt and pepper to taste

Step-by-Step Preparation:

1. Place the lentils, mushrooms, onion, and garlic in the slow cooker.
2. Pour in the vegetable broth.
3. Add the thyme, rosemary, salt, and pepper.
4. Stir to combine the ingredients.
5. Cover and cook on low for 6 hours until the lentils are tender.
6. Adjust seasoning as needed before serving.

Nutritional Facts: (Per serving)

- Calories: 280
- Carbohydrates: 49g
- Protein: 18g
- Fat: 1g
- Fiber: 18g
- Sugar: 5g

Relish the simplicity and depth of this Mushroom Vegan Lentil Stew, a dish that brings nutrition and comfort to your table. It's ideal for a cozy night, providing a warm, delicious, and effortlessly prepared meal.

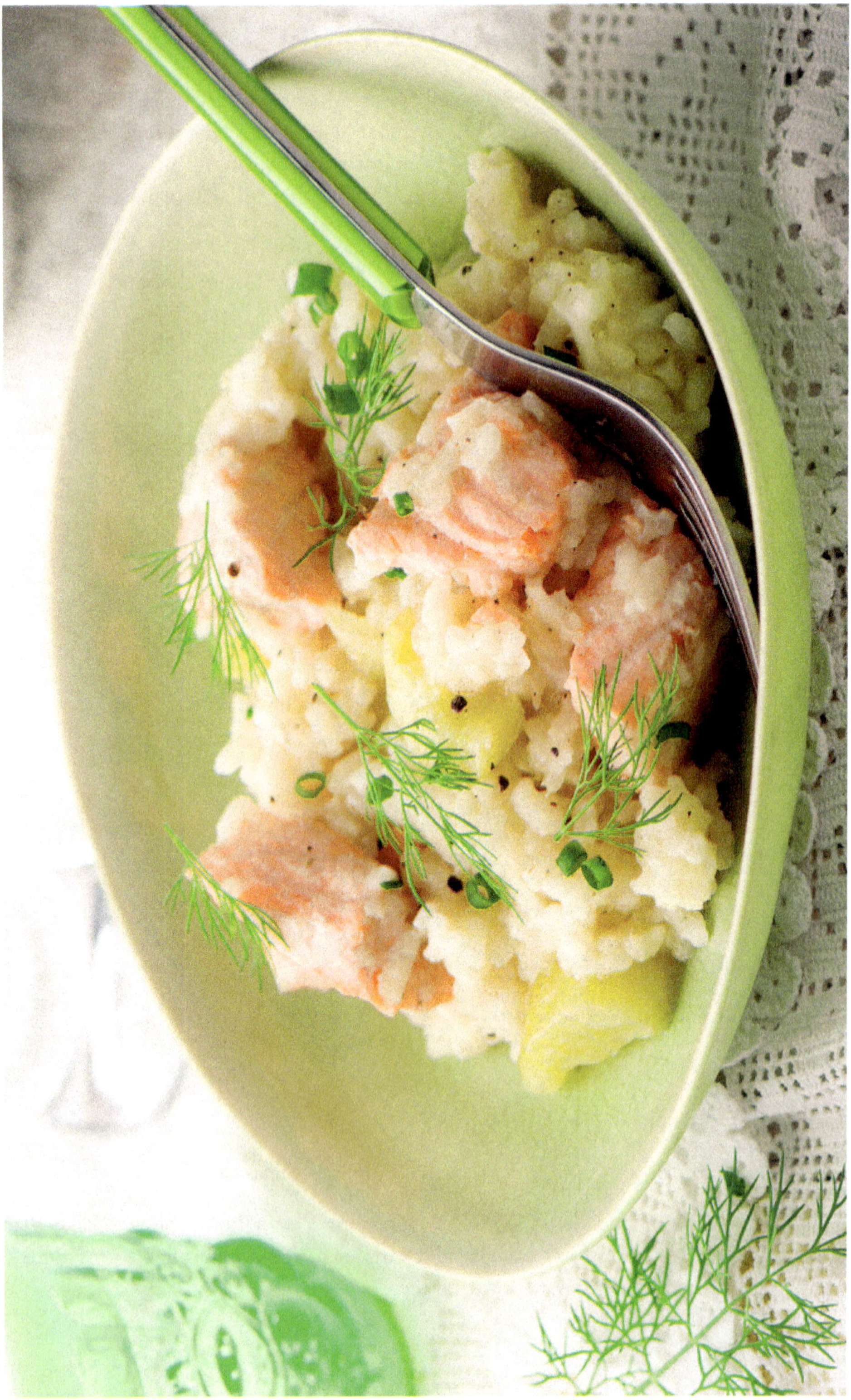

Chapter 04: Seafood Solo

Recipe 31: Slow Cooker Salmon Risotto

Dive into the luxurious world of seafood with this Slow Cooker Salmon Risotto, a dish that elegantly combines the richness of salmon with creamy risotto. This recipe simplifies gourmet cooking, bringing a sophisticated and hearty meal to your table with the ease of a slow cooker, perfect for a solo indulgence.

Servings: 1

Prepping Time: 10 minutes

Cook Time: 2 hours

Difficulty: Medium

Ingredients:

- ½ cup Arborio rice
- 1 small salmon fillet
- 1 ½ cups fish or vegetable broth
- ¼ cup white wine
- 1 small onion, finely chopped
- 1 garlic clove, minced
- 1 tbsp olive oil
- 2 tbsp grated Parmesan cheese
- Salt and pepper to taste
- Fresh parsley for garnish

Step-by-Step Preparation:

1. Heat olive oil in a pan and sauté onion and garlic until soft.
2. Add Arborio rice, stirring for 1 minute.
3. Transfer the mixture to the slow cooker.
4. Pour in broth and white wine.
5. Season the salmon with salt and pepper and place it on top of the rice.
6. Cover and cook on low for 2 hours.
7. Gently flake the salmon and stir into the risotto.
8. Mix in Parmesan cheese.
9. Garnish with fresh parsley before serving.

Nutritional Facts: (Per serving)

- Calories: 510
- Carbohydrates: 58g
- Protein: 25g
- Fat: 18g
- Fiber: 2g
- Sugar: 3g

This Slow Cooker Salmon Risotto is a testament to the beauty of combining simple ingredients to create a comforting and elegant dish. Perfect for a night when you crave something special, it brings a touch of gourmet to your home dining experience.

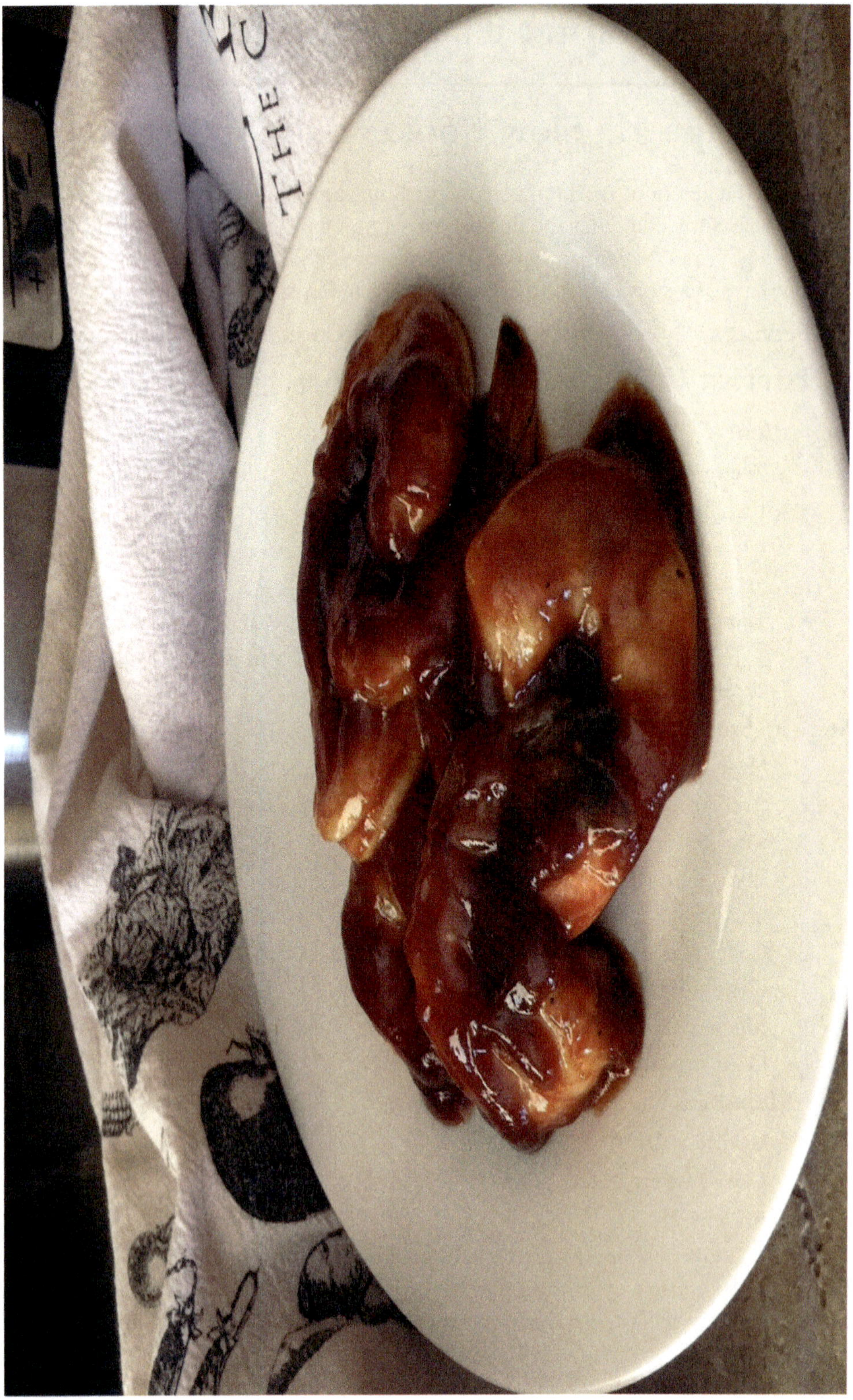

Recipe 32: BBQ Shrimp

Immerse yourself in the bold and smoky flavors of BBQ Shrimp, a simple yet irresistible slow cooker dish. This recipe is perfect for seafood lovers seeking a hassle-free, delicious meal. Combining juicy shrimp with a rich BBQ sauce is an easy way to enjoy a classic favorite with minimal effort.

Servings: 1

Prepping Time: 10 minutes

Cook Time: 2 hours

Difficulty: Easy

Ingredients:

- 10 large shrimp, peeled and deveined
- ½ cup BBQ sauce
- 1 garlic clove, minced
- 1 tbsp lemon juice
- 1 tsp smoked paprika
- ½ tsp chili powder
- Salt and pepper to taste

Step-by-Step Preparation:

1. Mix BBQ sauce, garlic, lemon juice, smoked paprika, chili powder, salt, and pepper in a bowl.
2. Add the shrimp to the sauce mixture and stir to coat evenly.
3. Place the shrimp and sauce in the slow cooker.
4. Cook on low for 2 hours.
5. Serve the shrimp with extra sauce from the cooker.

Nutritional Facts: (Per serving)

- Calories: 230
- Carbohydrates: 28g
- Protein: 24g
- Fat: 3g
- Saturated Fat: 0.5g
- Cholesterol: 180mg
- Sodium: 1200mg
- Fiber: 1g
- Sugar: 20g

Enjoy the comfort and ease of preparing this BBQ Shrimp, a dish that promises to satisfy your seafood cravings while keeping things simple and stress-free. It's the perfect recipe for a relaxed evening, offering a flavorful and delightful meal with minimal effort.

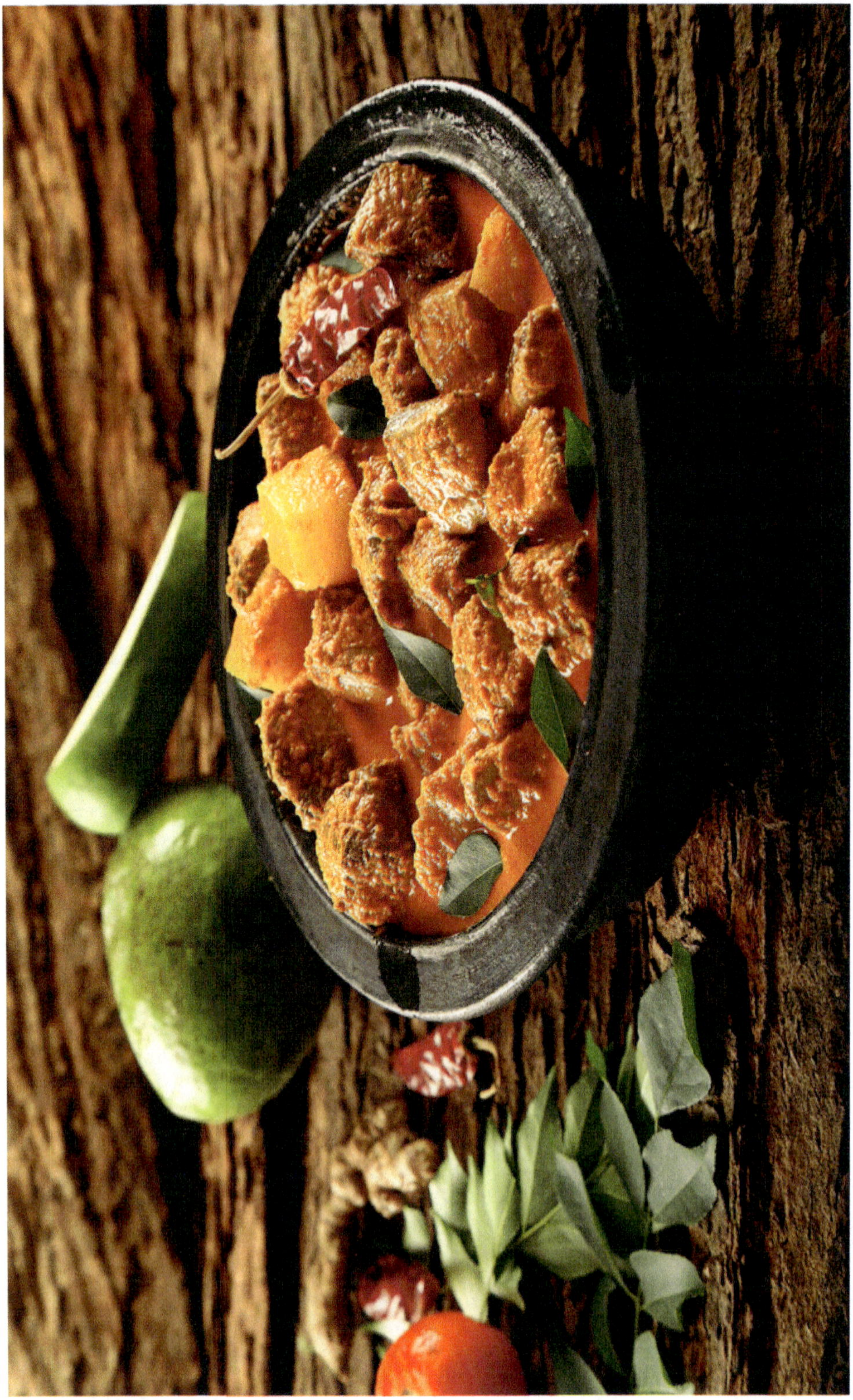

Recipe 33: Fish Curry with Mango

Dive into the exotic flavors of the tropics with this Fish Curry with Mango, a slow cooker dish that marries the richness of coconut milk with the tang of mango and a blend of aromatic spices. Ideal for seafood enthusiasts, this recipe offers a unique twist on traditional curry, creating a delightful, easy-to-prepare meal for one

Servings: 1

Prepping Time: 15 minutes

Cook Time: 3 hours

Difficulty: Medium

Ingredients:

- 1 fish fillet (like tilapia or cod)
- ½ cup coconut milk
- ½ ripe mango, diced
- 1 small onion, finely chopped
- 1 garlic clove, minced
- ½ tsp turmeric powder
- ½ tsp cumin powder
- ¼ tsp chili powder
- Salt to taste
- Fresh cilantro for garnish

Step-by-Step Preparation:

1. Place the fish fillet in the slow cooker.
2. Sprinkle turmeric, cumin, chili powder, and salt over the fish.
3. Add the chopped onion and minced garlic.
4. Pour coconut milk over the ingredients.
5. Scatter diced mango around the fish.
6. Cover and cook on low for 3 hours.
7. Carefully check if the fish is cooked through and tender.
8. Garnish with fresh cilantro before serving.

Nutritional Facts: (Per serving)

- Calories: 380
- Carbohydrates: 20g
- Protein: 25g
- Fat: 22g
- Saturated Fat: 15g
- Cholesterol: 60mg
- Sodium: 300mg
- Fiber: 2g
- Sugar: 12g

This Fish Curry with Mango in Coconut Milk is more than a meal; it's an adventure in flavors, bringing a slice of the tropics to your table. Perfect for a cozy night in, it offers a delightful escape to exotic culinary landscapes with every bite.

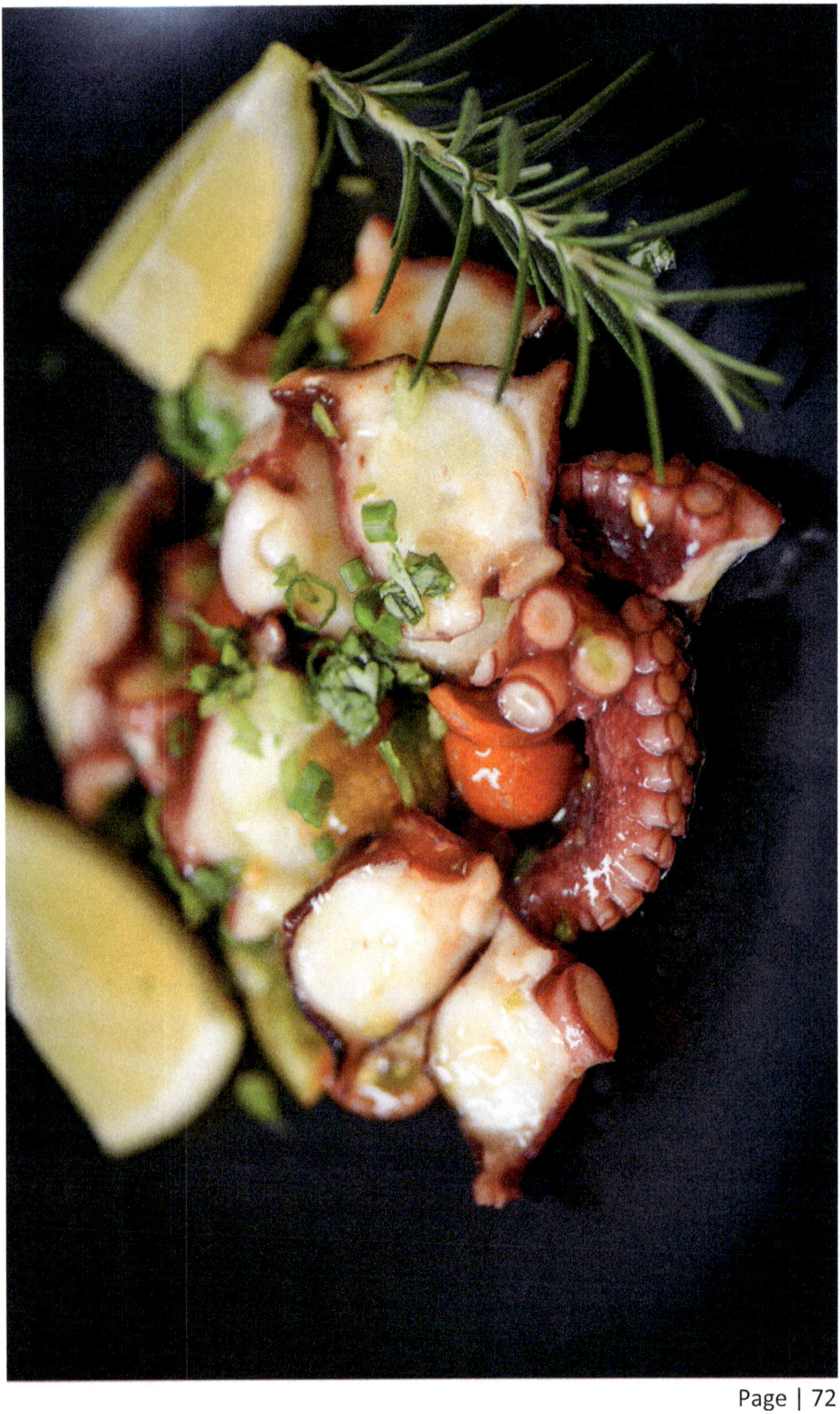

Recipe 34: Octopus Salad

Embark on a culinary adventure with this exquisite Octopus Salad, a vibrant blend of lemon, tomatoes, rosemary, and crisp vegetables. Perfectly cooked in a slow cooker, the octopus becomes tantalizingly tender, creating a refreshing and sophisticated seafood salad ideal for a gourmet solo meal.

Servings: 1

Prepping Time: 30 minutes

Cook Time: 4 hours

Difficulty: Intermediate

Ingredients:

- 1 small octopus (about 250g), cleaned
- 1 lemon, juiced and zested
- 1 ripe tomato, chopped
- 1 sprig of rosemary
- ½ cup mixed vegetables (such as bell peppers, cucumbers, and carrots), chopped
- 1 tbsp olive oil
- Salt and pepper to taste

Step-by-Step Preparation:

1. Place the octopus and rosemary in the slow cooker.
2. Add water until the octopus is fully submerged.
3. Cook on low for 4 hours until tender.
4. Once cooked, remove the octopus, let it cool, and then slice it into pieces.
5. Mix the chopped tomato, mixed vegetables, octopus, lemon juice, and zest in a bowl.
6. Drizzle with olive oil, and season with salt and pepper.
7. Toss gently to combine.
8. Refrigerate for 30 minutes before serving to enhance flavors.

Nutritional Facts: (Per serving)

- Calories: 320
- Carbohydrates: 20g
- Protein: 30g
- Fat: 12g
- Saturated Fat: 2g
- Cholesterol: 80mg
- Sodium: 500mg
- Fiber: 3g
- Sugar: 4g

This Octopus Salad celebrates sea flavors and garden-fresh ingredients, offering a light yet fulfilling meal. Its harmonious blend of textures and tastes makes it a perfect choice for a special yet easy-to-prepare lunch or dinner.

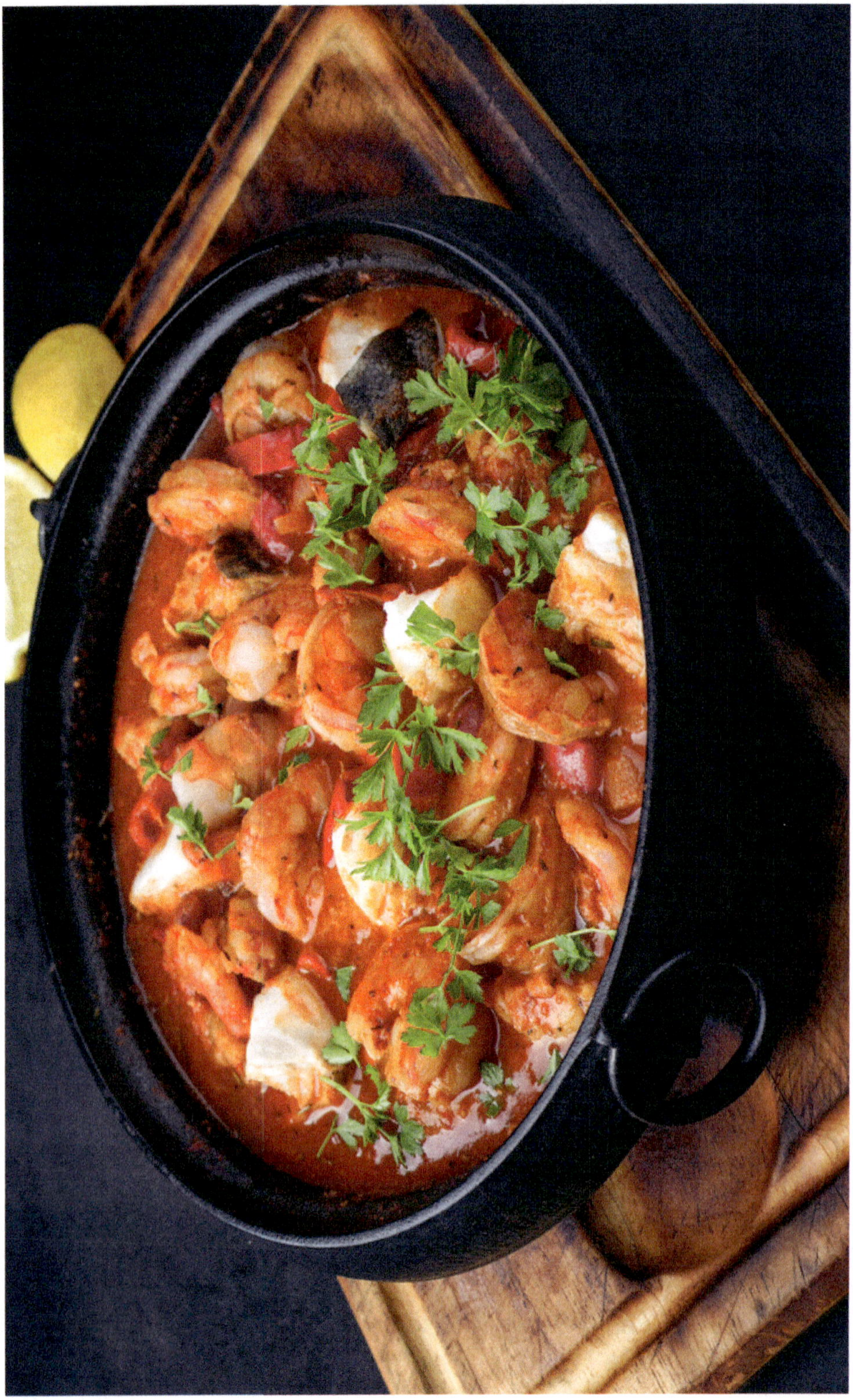

Recipe 35: American Fish Stew

Delight in the rich flavors of the sea with American Fish Stew Cioppino, a classic seafood medley that combines prawns and fish in a savory tomato broth. This slow cooker version simplifies the traditional recipe, making it an accessible yet luxurious dish for a solo seafood feast.

Servings: 1

Prepping Time: 20 minutes

Cook Time: 4 hours

Difficulty: Medium

Ingredients:

- 4 prawns, peeled and deveined
- 1 fish fillet (like cod or tilapia), cut into chunks
- 1 cup canned tomatoes, crushed
- 1 small onion, diced
- 1 garlic clove, minced
- ½ cup fish or vegetable broth
- 1 tsp olive oil
- ½ tsp dried basil
- ½ tsp dried oregano
- Salt and pepper to taste
- Fresh parsley for garnish

Step-by-Step Preparation:

1. Heat olive oil in a pan, sauté onion and garlic until soft.
2. Transfer to the slow cooker.
3. Add crushed tomatoes, broth, basil, oregano, salt, and pepper.
4. Stir to combine.
5. Add the fish chunks and prawns.
6. Cover and cook on low for 4 hours.
7. Check if the seafood is cooked through.
8. Garnish with fresh parsley before serving.

Nutritional Facts: (Per serving)

- Calories: 350
- Carbohydrates: 20g
- Protein: 40g
- Fat: 12g
- Saturated Fat: 2g
- Cholesterol: 180mg
- Sodium: 700mg
- Fiber: 3g
- Sugar: 6g

This American Fish Stew Cioppino is a delightful way to enjoy a variety of seafood in one dish. Its rich, tomato-based broth brimming with succulent prawns and tender fish makes for a luxurious yet easy meal, perfect for a cozy night.

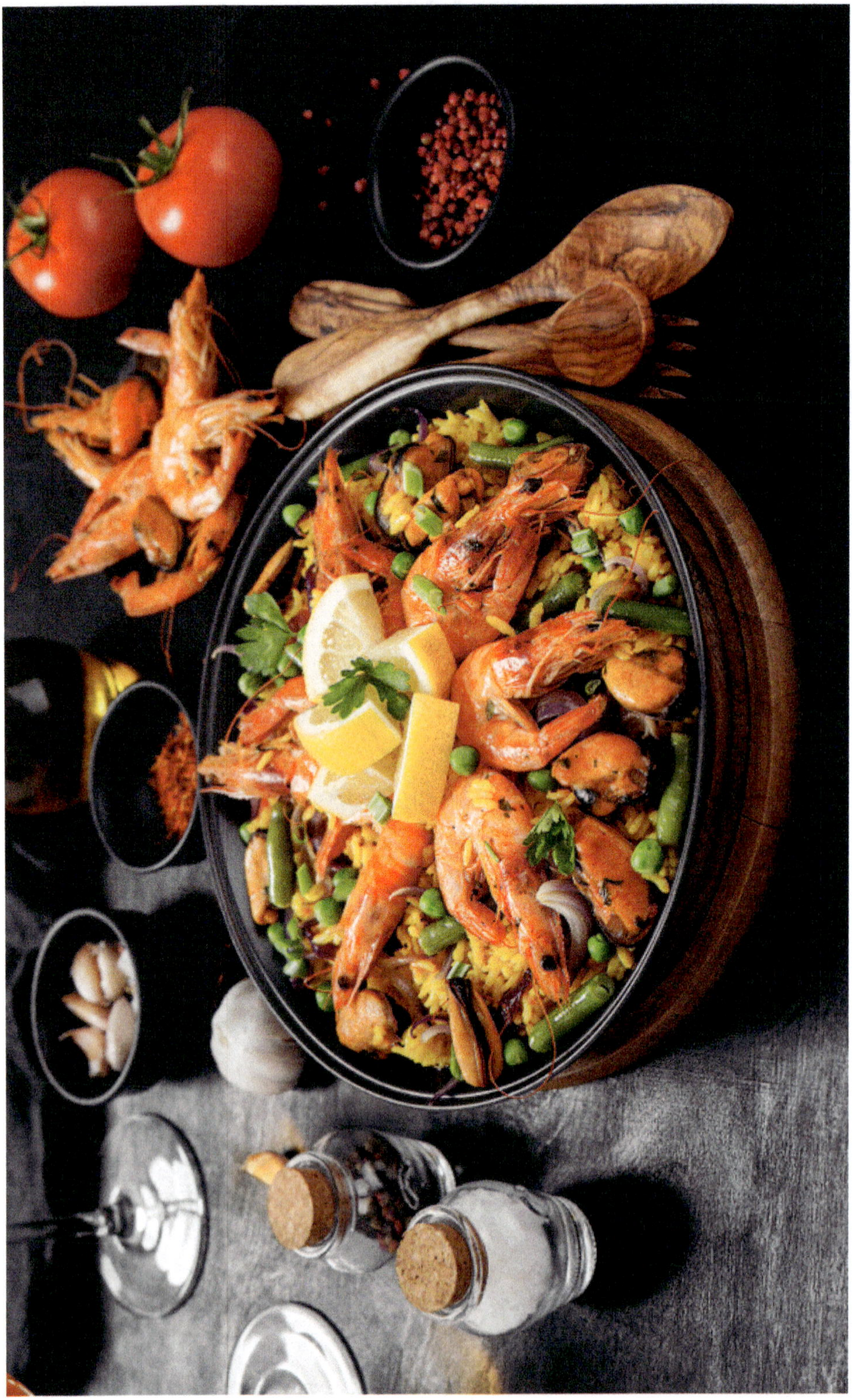

Recipe 36: Spanish Seafood Paella

Immerse yourself in the vibrant flavors of Spain with this Slow Cooker Spanish Seafood Paella. A single-serving delight, this dish is a symphony of seafood, aromatic spices, and rice, all cooked to perfection. Ideal for anyone craving a taste of the Mediterranean, it brings the essence of Spanish cuisine to your kitchen.

Servings: 1

Prepping Time: 15 minutes

Cook Time: 2 hours

Difficulty: Medium

Ingredients:
- ½ cup paella rice or short-grain rice
- 4 prawns, peeled and deveined
- 4 mussels, cleaned
- ½ cup chicken or fish broth
- ¼ cup diced tomatoes
- 1 garlic clove, minced
- ¼ onion, finely chopped
- 1 tsp olive oil
- ¼ tsp smoked paprika
- Pinch of saffron
- Salt and pepper to taste
- Lemon wedge and fresh parsley for garnish

Step-by-Step Preparation:
1. Heat olive oil in the slow cooker and sauté onion and garlic.
2. Add rice, stirring to coat with the oil.
3. Pour in broth and diced tomatoes.
4. Add smoked paprika, saffron, salt, and pepper.
5. Arrange prawns and mussels on top of the rice.
6. Cook on low for 2 hours, until rice is tender and seafood is cooked.
7. Let it rest for a few minutes.
8. Garnish with a lemon wedge and fresh parsley before serving.

Nutritional Facts: (Per serving)
- Calories: 400
- Carbohydrates: 58g
- Protein: 25g
- Fat: 10g
- Saturated Fat: 1.5g
- Cholesterol: 120mg
- Sodium: 700mg
- Fiber: 3g
- Sugar: 4g

This Spanish Seafood Paella in a slow cooker is a delightful escape into a world of flavorful seafood and aromatic spices. It's perfect for when you're yearning for something exotic yet comforting, bringing the taste of Spain to your solo dining experience.

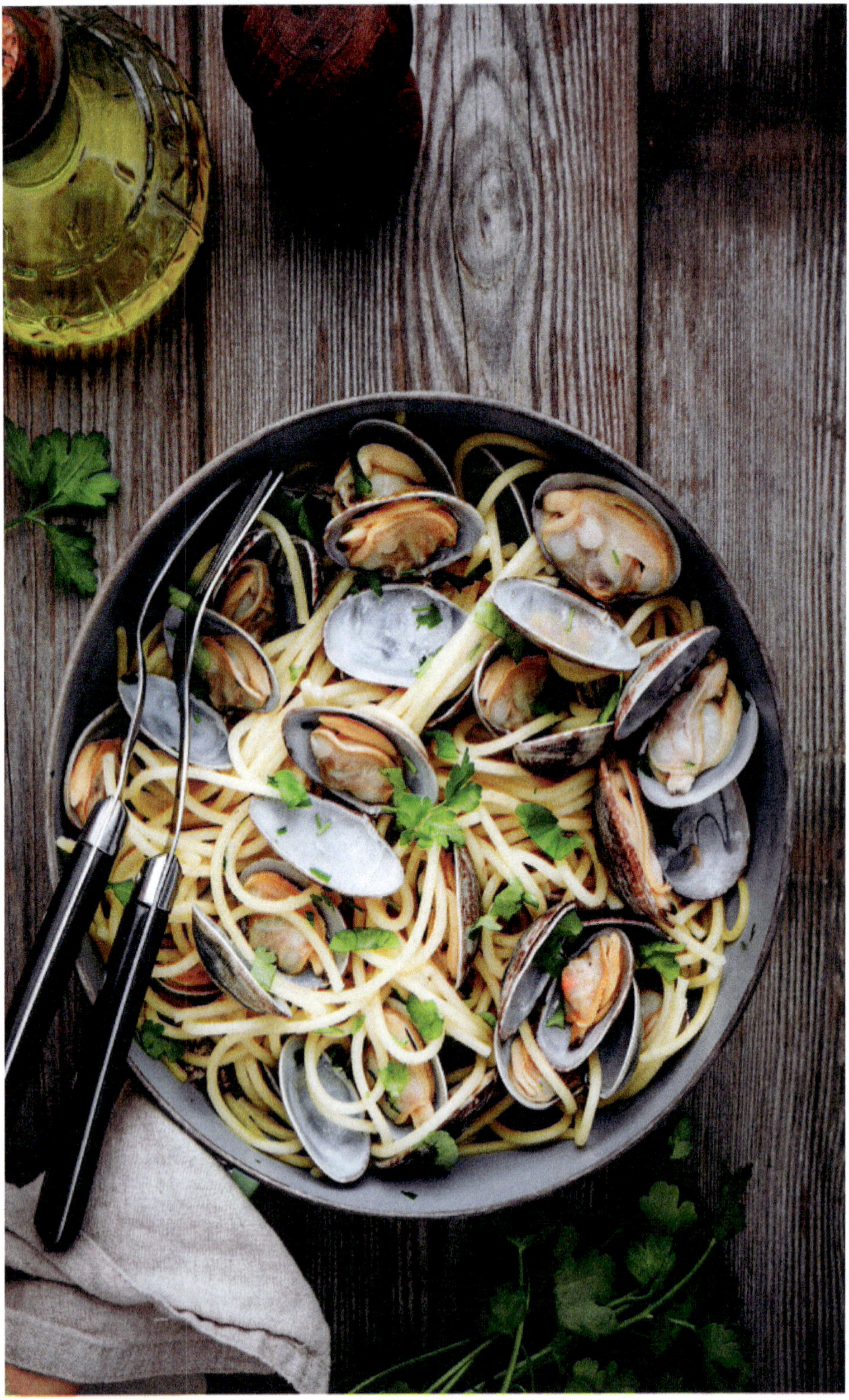

Recipe 37: Italian Seafood Pasta

Indulge in the classic Italian charm of Spaghetti alle Vongole, a delightful seafood pasta featuring tender clams. This slow cooker adaptation simplifies the traditional preparation, making it perfect for a luxurious single-serving meal. Enjoy the harmonious blend of simple ingredients and the rich flavors of the sea, all coming together to create an exquisite dining experience.

Servings: 1

Prepping Time: 20 minutes

Cook Time: 2 hours

Difficulty: Easy

Ingredients:

- ½ cup spaghetti
- 1 cup clams, cleaned
- 1 garlic clove, minced
- ½ cup white wine
- 1 tbsp olive oil
- 1 small tomato, diced
- Pinch of red pepper flakes
- Salt and pepper to taste
- Fresh parsley, chopped for garnish

Step-by-Step Preparation:

1. Place the spaghetti in the slow cooker.
2. Add clams, minced garlic, and diced tomato.
3. Pour in white wine and olive oil.
4. Sprinkle with red pepper flakes, salt, and pepper.
5. Cover and cook on low for 2 hours or until pasta is al dente, and the clams have opened.
6. Discard any clams that haven't opened.
7. Garnish with fresh parsley before serving.

Nutritional Facts: (Per serving)

- Calories: 460
- Carbohydrates: 42g
- Protein: 22g
- Fat: 18g
- Saturated Fat: 2.5g
- Cholesterol: 50mg
- Sodium: 300mg
- Fiber: 2g
- Sugar: 3g

Savor the essence of Italian coastal cuisine with this simple yet elegant Spaghetti alle Vongole. It's a perfect dish for those seeking a taste of Italy's seafood delicacies, offering a comforting and satisfying meal that's easy to prepare and delightful to enjoy.

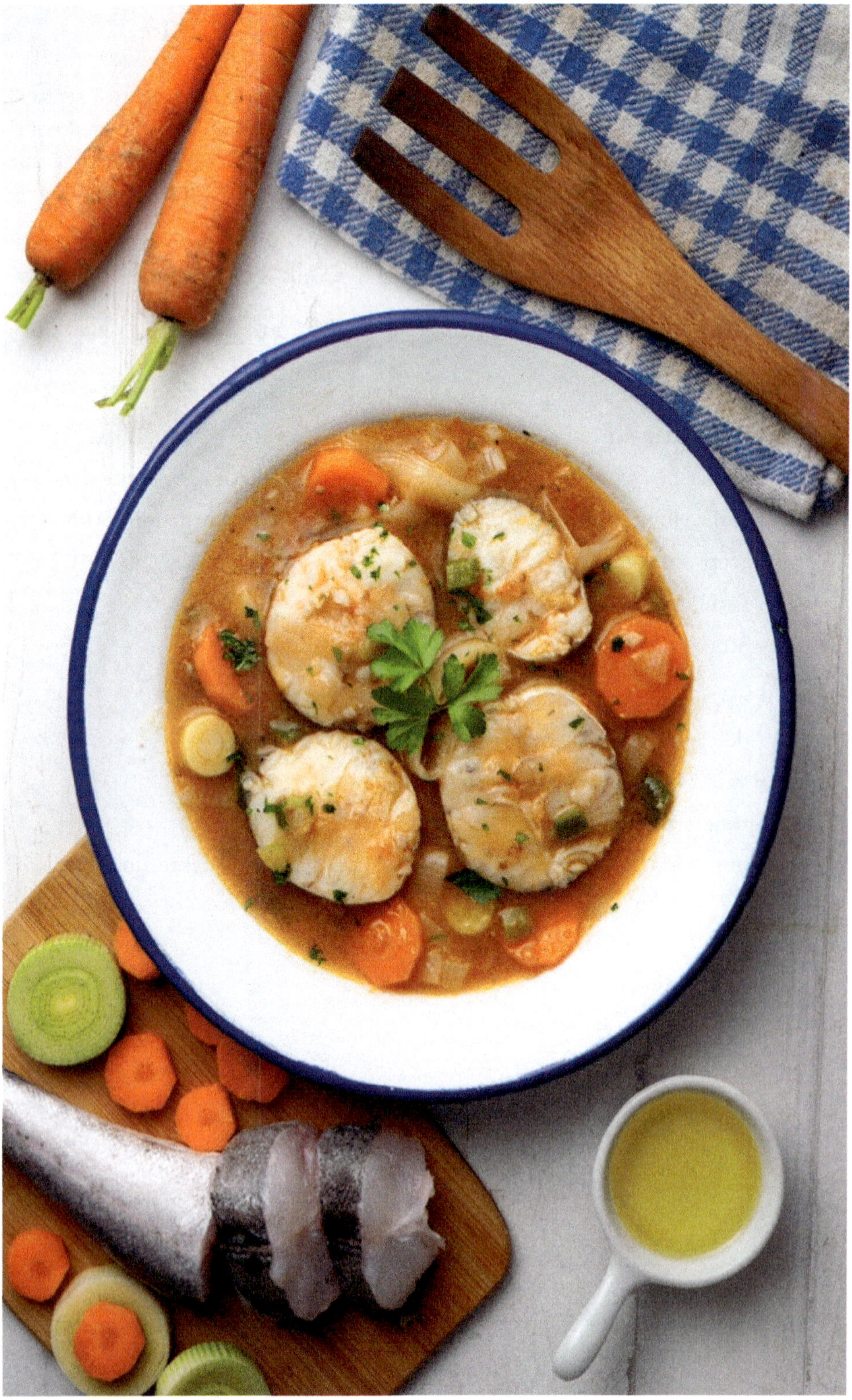

Recipe 38: Hake Stew with Potatoes

Savor the simplicity and heartiness of this Hake Stew, a delightful slow cooker fish dish that combines tender hake with potatoes, leeks, and various seasonal vegetables. This one-pot wonder is a testament to the comfort and flavors that can be coaxed from simple, fresh ingredients, making it an ideal meal for any seafood lover.

Servings: 1

Prepping Time: 15 minutes

Cook Time: 4 hours

Difficulty: Easy

Ingredients:

- 1 hake fillet
- 1 small potato, diced
- ½ leek, sliced
- ½ cup mixed seasonal vegetables (like carrots, celery, bell peppers)
- 1 garlic clove, minced
- 1 cup fish or vegetable broth
- ½ tsp dried thyme
- Salt and pepper to taste
- Fresh parsley, chopped for garnish

Step-by-Step Preparation:

1. Place the diced potato, sliced leek, and mixed vegetables in the slow cooker.
2. Add minced garlic and dried thyme.
3. Pour in the broth and season with salt and pepper.
4. Place the hake fillet on top of the vegetables.
5. Cover and cook on low for 4 hours until the fish is cooked through and the vegetables are tender.
6. Gently break the hake into pieces and stir into the stew.
7. Garnish with fresh parsley before serving.

Nutritional Facts: (Per serving)

- Calories: 320
- Carbohydrates: 38g
- Protein: 28g
- Fat: 6g
- Saturated Fat: 1g
- Cholesterol: 60mg
- Sodium: 700mg
- Fiber: 5g
- Sugar: 5g

With its blend of succulent fish and wholesome vegetables, this Hake Stew is a nourishing and comforting meal, perfect for those chilly evenings or whenever you crave a touch of home-cooked goodness. It's a simple yet flavorful dish celebrating the best seasonal produce and fresh seafood.

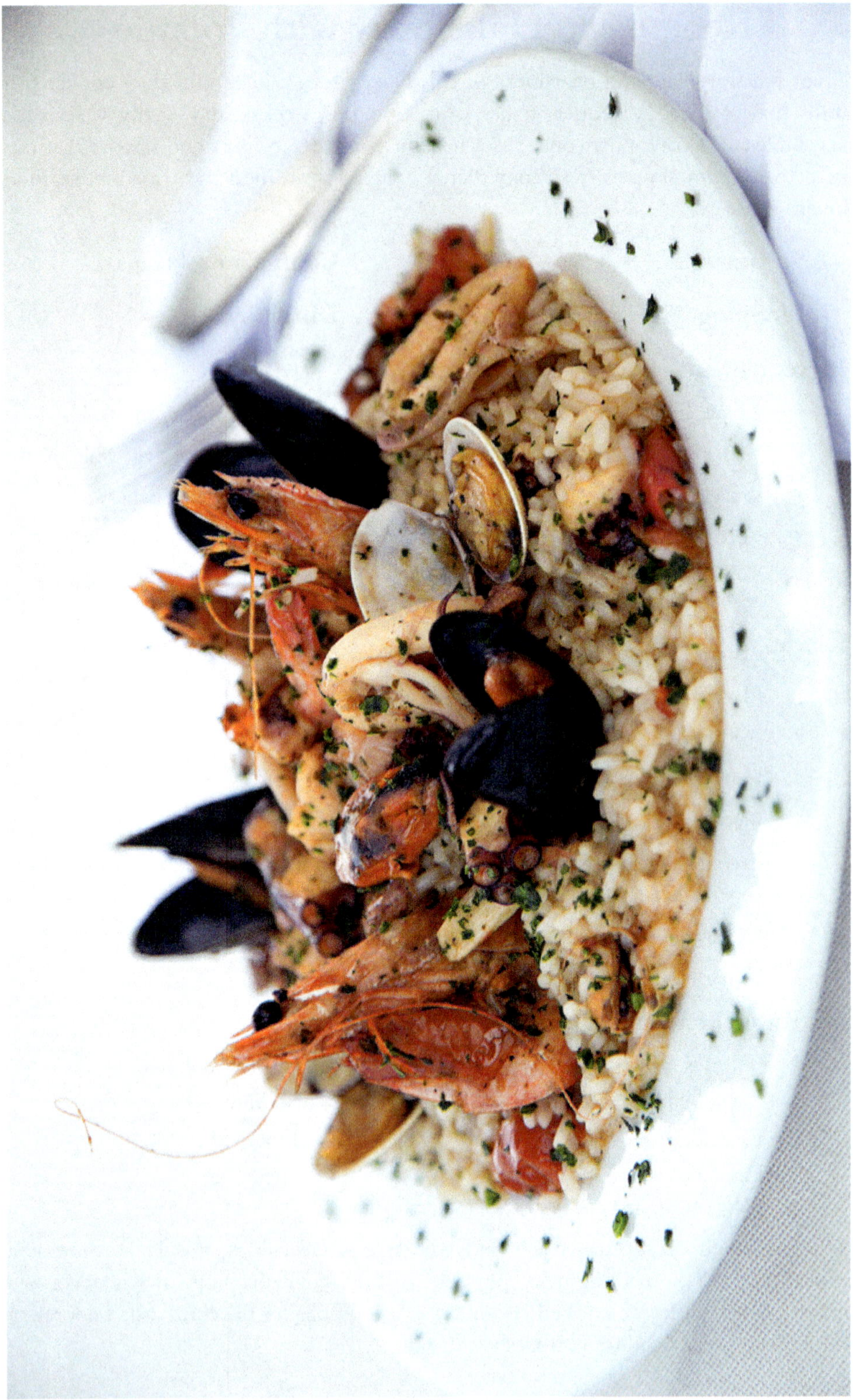

Recipe 39: Italian Risotto

Embark on a culinary voyage to Italy with this exquisite Italian Risotto, brimming with a luxurious assortment of shrimp, mussels, octopus, and clams, complemented by the sweetness of tomatoes. This slow cooker seafood dish offers a hassle-free way to enjoy the lavish flavors of a traditional Italian risotto, perfect for a sumptuous solo dining experience.

Servings: 1

Prepping Time: 20 minutes

Cook Time: 2 hours

Difficulty: Medium

Ingredients:

- ½ cup Arborio rice
- 4 shrimps, peeled and deveined
- 4 mussels, cleaned
- 1 small octopus, cleaned and cut into pieces
- 4 clams, cleaned
- 1 cup diced tomatoes
- 1 garlic clove, minced
- 1 small onion, finely chopped
- 2 cups fish stock
- 1 tbsp olive oil
- Salt and pepper to taste
- Fresh parsley, chopped for garnish

Step-by-Step Preparation:

1. Heat olive oil in the slow cooker, sauté onion and garlic.
2. Add Arborio rice, stirring to coat with the oil.
3. Pour in fish stock and diced tomatoes.
4. Season with salt and pepper.
5. Add shrimp, mussels, octopus' pieces, and clams.
6. Cover and cook on low for 2 hours, until the rice is creamy and seafood is cooked.
7. Discard any mussels or clams that didn't open.
8. Garnish with fresh parsley before serving.

Nutritional Facts: (Per serving)

- Calories: 510
- Carbohydrates: 58g
- Protein: 40g
- Fat: 14g
- Saturated Fat: 2g
- Cholesterol: 120mg
- Sodium: 800mg
- Fiber: 3g
- Sugar: 5g

With its rich seafood medley and creamy texture, this Italian Risotto is a delightful treat for any seafood lover. It's a testament to the art of slow cooking, transforming simple ingredients into a gourmet meal that's both satisfying and luxurious.

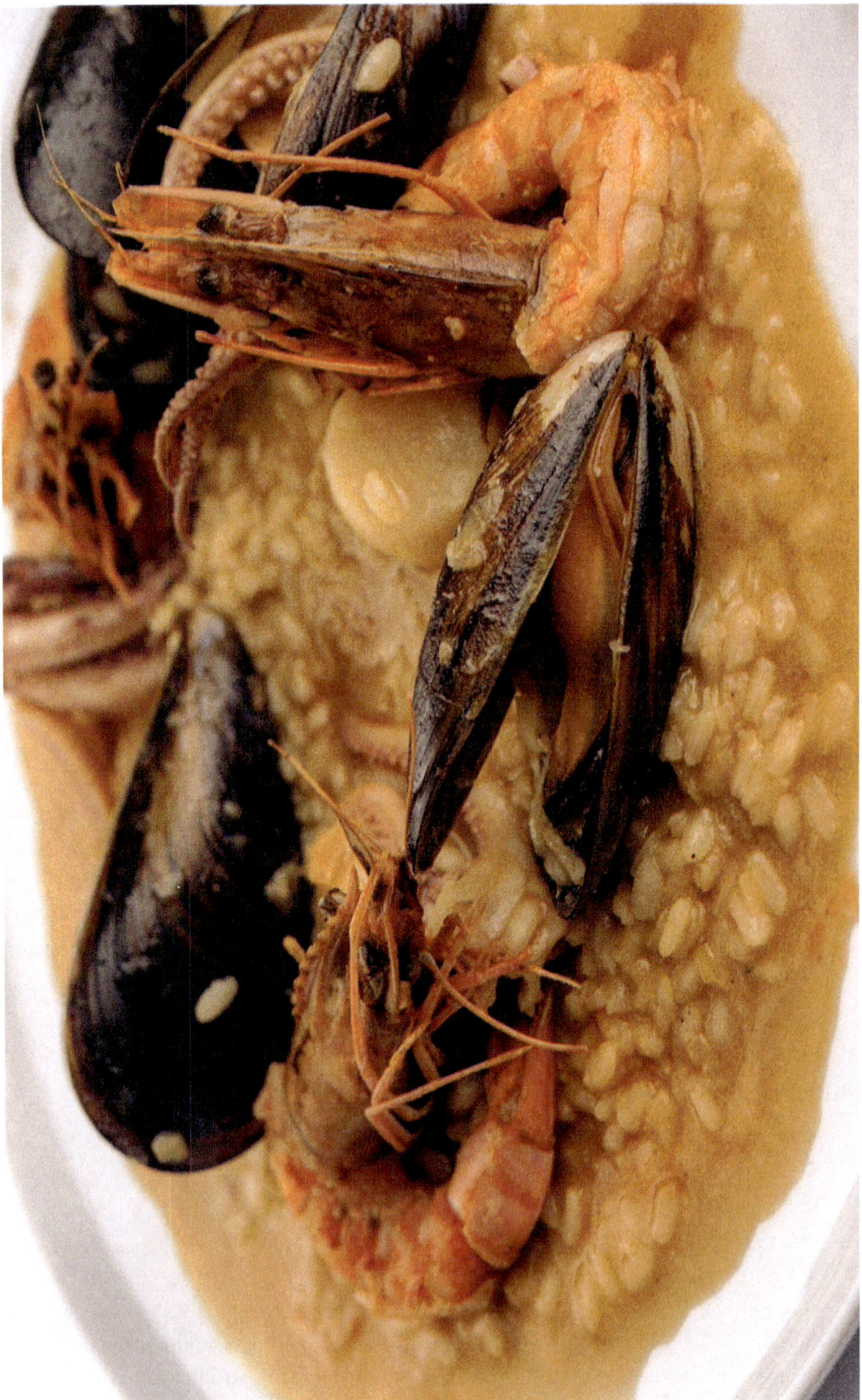

Recipe 40: Seafood Risotto with Mussel Shrimp and Squid

Experience the essence of the ocean with this Seafood Risotto, a delightful slow-cooker dish that melds the flavors of mussels, shrimp, and squid. This recipe simplifies the traditional risotto process, perfect for seafood aficionados, resulting in a creamy, flavorful, and easy-to-make meal that's ideal for a luxurious solo dining experience.

Servings: 1

Prepping Time: 20 minutes

Cook Time: 2 hours

Difficulty: Medium

Ingredients:

- ½ cup Arborio rice
- 4 mussels, cleaned
- 4 shrimps, peeled and deveined
- 1 small squid, cleaned and sliced
- 1 garlic clove, minced
- 1 small onion, finely chopped
- 2 cups fish stock
- 1 tbsp olive oil
- Salt and pepper to taste
- Fresh parsley, chopped for garnish

Step-by-Step Preparation:

1. Heat olive oil in the slow cooker, sauté onion and garlic.
2. Add Arborio rice, stirring to coat well.
3. Pour in fish stock.
4. Season with salt and pepper.
5. Add mussels, shrimp, and squid.
6. Cover and cook on low for 2 hours, until rice is creamy and seafood is cooked.
7. Discard any mussels that didn't open.
8. Garnish with fresh parsley before serving.

Nutritional Facts: (Per serving)

- Calories: 500
- Carbohydrates: 56g
- Protein: 38g
- Fat: 13g
- Saturated Fat: 2g
- Cholesterol: 115mg
- Sodium: 800mg
- Fiber: 2g
- Sugar: 4g

This Seafood Risotto, with its harmonious blend of mussels, shrimp, and squid, offers a taste of the sea in every bite. It's a perfect choice for those seeking to enjoy the finesse of Italian cooking in a simple yet sophisticated and satisfying meal.

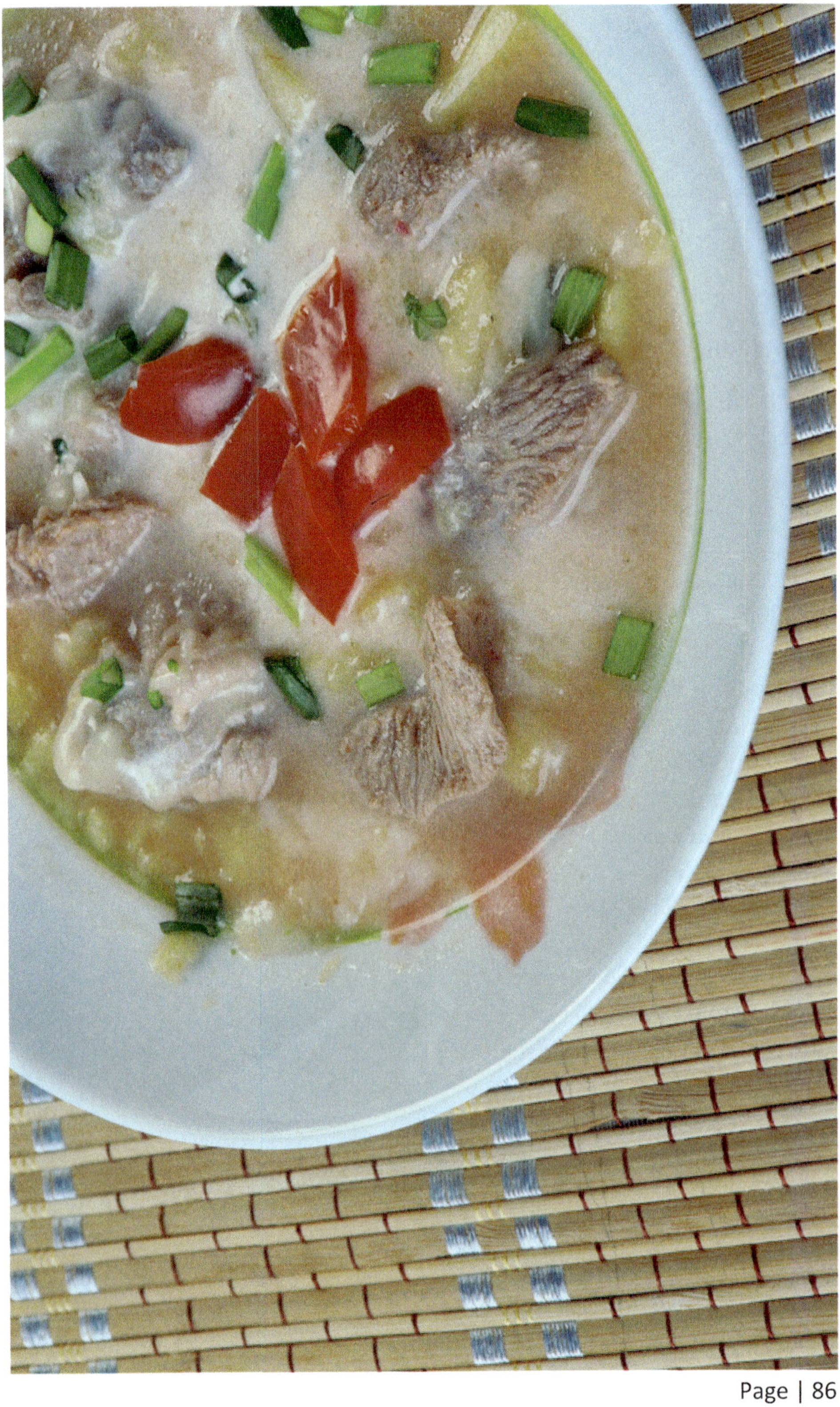

Chapter 05: Snackable Moments

Recipe 41: King Ranch Chicken Soup

Immerse yourself in the comforting embrace of Texan cuisine with King Ranch Chicken Soup, a slow-cooker dish that's hearty and flavorful. This recipe transforms the classic King Ranch casserole into a soul-warming soup, perfect for a cozy meal. It's a simple yet deliciously satisfying way to enjoy a Texan favorite in a new, soup-based form.

Servings: 1

Prepping Time: 10 minutes

Cook Time: 4 hours

Difficulty: Easy

Ingredients:

- 1 chicken breast, diced
- 1 cup chicken broth
- ¼ cup diced tomatoes with green chilies
- ¼ onion, chopped
- 1 garlic clove, minced
- ½ cup cream of chicken soup
- ¼ cup shredded cheddar cheese
- ½ tsp cumin
- Salt and pepper to taste
- Crushed tortilla chips for garnish

Step-by-Step Preparation:

1. Place the diced chicken breast in the slow cooker.
2. Add chicken broth, diced tomatoes with green chilies, chopped onion, and minced garlic.
3. Stir in cream of chicken soup, cumin, salt, and pepper.
4. Cover and cook on low for 4 hours until the chicken is tender.
5. Stir in shredded cheddar cheese until melted and well combined.
6. Serve hot, garnished with crushed tortilla chips.

Nutritional Facts: (Per serving)

- Calories: 380
- Carbohydrates: 18g
- Protein: 33g
- Fat: 20g
- Saturated Fat: 9g
- Cholesterol: 95mg
- Sodium: 1200mg
- Fiber: 2g
- Sugar: 4g

Enjoy the warmth and richness of this King Ranch Chicken Soup, a dish that offers all the flavors of a beloved Texan casserole in a comforting and easy-to-prepare soup form. Perfect for a relaxed night in, it's a taste of home with every spoonful.

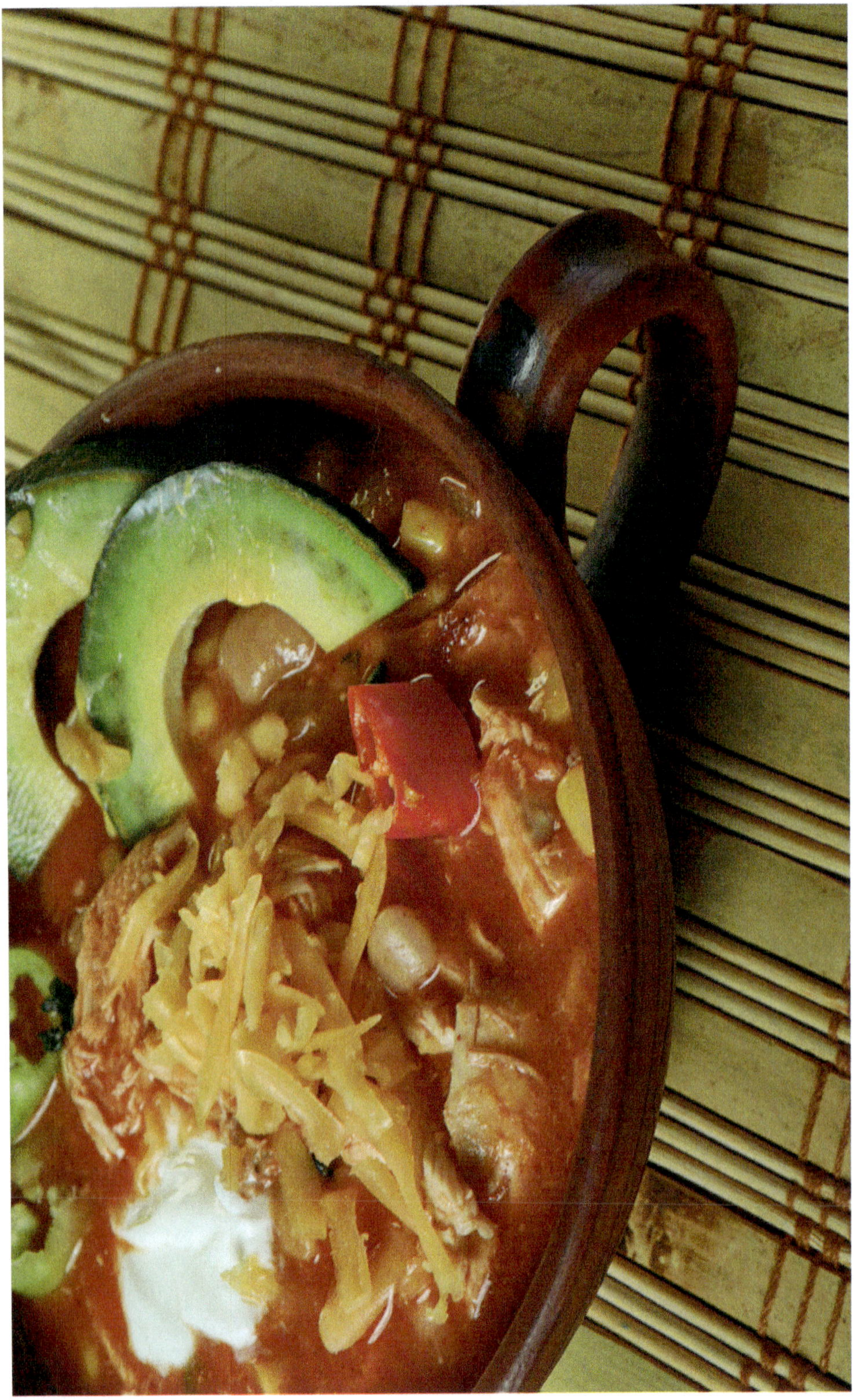

Recipe 42: Mexican Fiesta Chicken Soup

Embark on a flavorful journey with Mexican Fiesta Chicken Soup, a vibrant and hearty slow cooker dish that captures the essence of Mexican cuisine. Ideal for anyone seeking a comforting yet zesty meal, this soup combines tender chicken with a medley of spices and vegetables, creating a delightful and easy-to-prepare feast for the senses.

Servings: 1

Prepping Time: 15 minutes

Cook Time: 6 hours

Difficulty: Easy

Ingredients:

- 1 chicken breast, diced
- 1 cup chicken broth
- ½ cup canned black beans rinsed and drained
- ½ cup corn kernels
- ¼ cup diced tomatoes
- ¼ onion, chopped
- 1 garlic clove, minced
- ½ tsp chili powder
- ½ tsp cumin
- Salt and pepper to taste
- Fresh cilantro and lime wedge for garnish

Step-by-Step Preparation:

1. Place the diced chicken breast in the slow cooker.
2. Add chicken broth, black beans, corn, diced tomatoes, onion, and garlic.
3. Season with chili powder, cumin, salt, and pepper.
4. Cover and cook on low for 6 hours until the chicken is tender.
5. Adjust seasoning as needed.
6. Serve hot, garnished with fresh cilantro and a squeeze of lime.

Nutritional Facts: (Per serving)

- Calories: 350
- Carbohydrates: 35g
- Protein: 36g
- Fat: 6g
- Saturated Fat: 1g
- Cholesterol: 65mg
- Sodium: 900mg
- Fiber: 10g
- Sugar: 5g

Relish the bold and lively flavors of this Mexican Fiesta Chicken Soup, which brings a fiesta of taste to your table. It's the perfect choice for a cozy evening, offering a nutritious and deliciously satisfying meal that's as enjoyable to prepare as it is to eat.

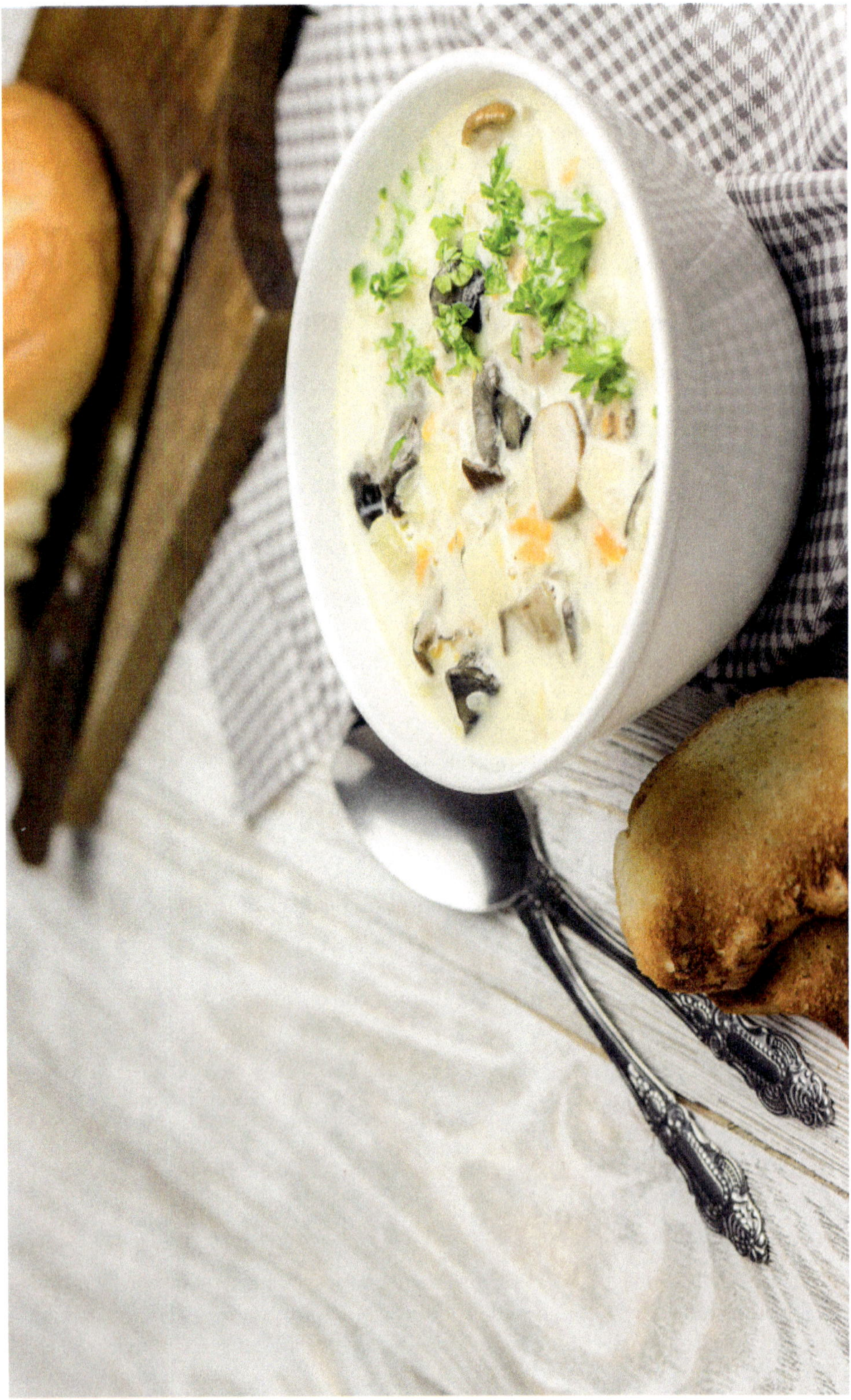

Recipe 43: Mushroom Soup

Delve into the earthy, comforting flavors of Mushroom Soup, a classic slow cooker dish designed for a cozy, nourishing meal. This recipe brings out the best in mushrooms, creating a rich, creamy, simple, and profoundly satisfying soup. It's perfect for anyone who loves the warm, umami flavors of mushrooms in a hearty, easy-to-prepare soup.

Servings: 1

Prepping Time: 10 minutes

Cook Time: 4 hours

Difficulty: Easy

Ingredients:

- 1 cup mushrooms, sliced
- 1 garlic clove, minced
- 1 small onion, chopped
- 1 cup vegetable broth
- ¼ cup heavy cream or coconut milk
- ½ tsp dried thyme
- Salt and pepper to taste
- Fresh parsley for garnish

Step-by-Step Preparation:

1. Place sliced mushrooms, garlic, and onion in the slow cooker.
2. Pour in vegetable broth.
3. Season with dried thyme, salt, and pepper.
4. Cover and cook on low for 4 hours.
5. Blend the soup to your desired consistency using an immersion blender.
6. Stir in heavy cream or coconut milk.
7. Heat through for an additional 10 minutes.
8. Serve hot, garnished with fresh parsley.

Nutritional Facts: (Per serving)

- Calories: 200
- Carbohydrates: 15g
- Protein: 4g
- Fat: 14g
- Saturated Fat: 8g
- Cholesterol: 40mg
- Sodium: 900mg
- Fiber: 2g
- Sugar: 6g

This Mushroom Soup is a delightful way to enjoy a warm, comforting meal. It's perfect for those chilly days when you crave something soothing and flavorful, offering a delectable blend of ingredients nourishing the body and soul.

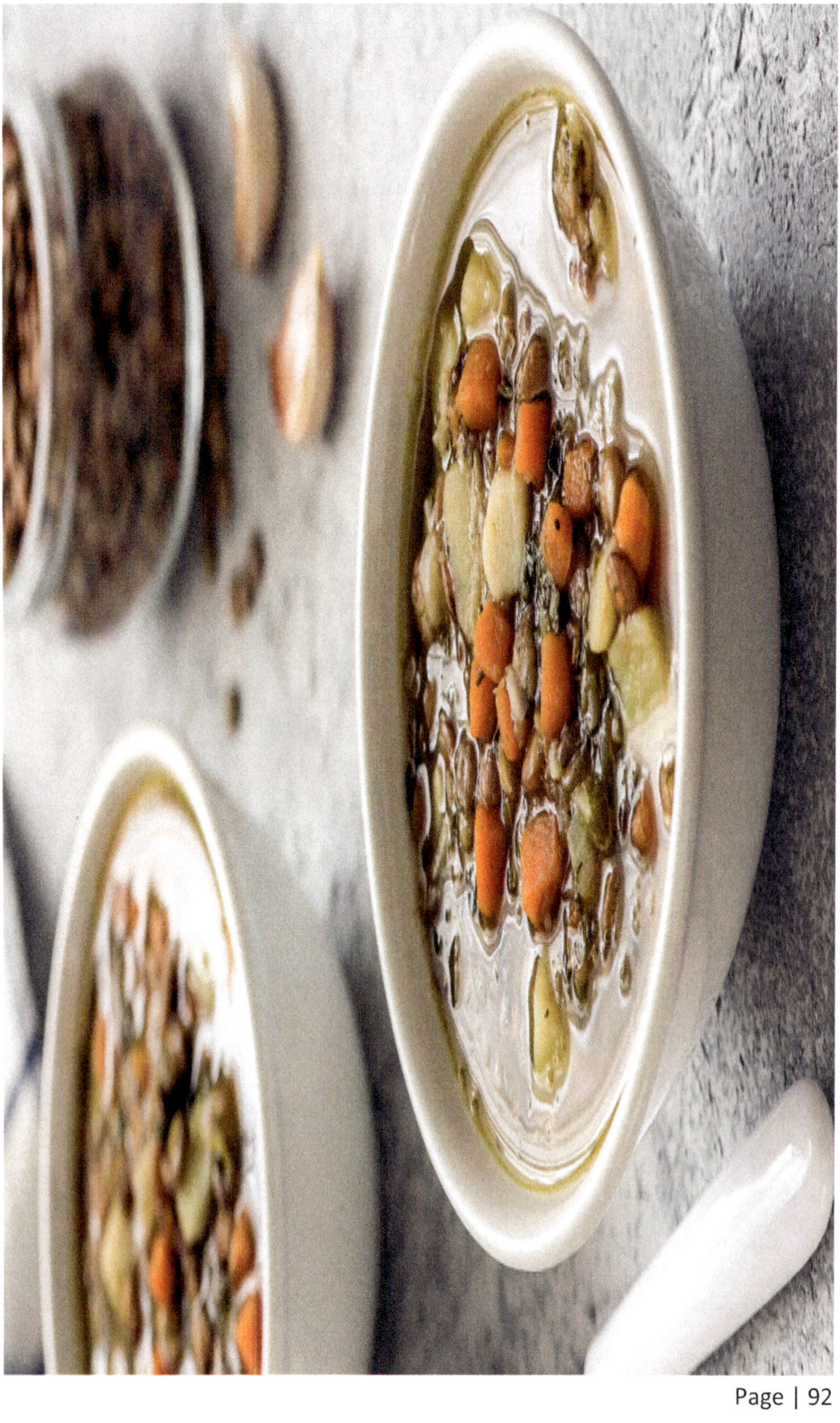

Recipe 44: Lentil Spinach Soup

Experience the hearty and nourishing flavors of Lentil Spinach Soup, a perfect slow cooker dish for health-conscious individuals. This simple yet delicious soup combines the wholesome goodness of lentils with the freshness of spinach, creating a comforting and nutrient-rich meal ideal for any time of the day.

Servings: 1

Prepping Time: 10 minutes

Cook Time: 6 hours

Difficulty: Easy

Ingredients:

- ½ cup dry lentils, rinsed
- 1 cup fresh spinach, chopped
- 1 small carrot, diced
- ½ small onion, chopped
- 1 garlic clove, minced
- 2 cups vegetable broth
- ½ tsp cumin
- Salt and pepper to taste

Step-by-Step Preparation:

1. Place lentils, carrots, onion, and garlic in the slow cooker.
2. Pour in vegetable broth.
3. Season with cumin, salt, and pepper.
4. Cover and cook on low for 6 hours until lentils are tender.
5. Stir in chopped spinach and cook for an additional 10 minutes until wilted.
6. Adjust seasoning if necessary and serve hot.

Nutritional Facts: (Per serving)

- Calories: 230
- Carbohydrates: 40g
- Protein: 18g
- Fat: 1g
- Saturated Fat: 0g
- Cholesterol: 0mg
- Sodium: 800mg
- Fiber: 18g
- Sugar: 4g

This Lentil Spinach Soup is a testament to the power of simple ingredients coming together to create a flavorsome and fulfilling meal. It's ideal for a cozy night in, offering a delicious way to enjoy a healthy, plant-based dish that's as easy to prepare as it is satisfying.

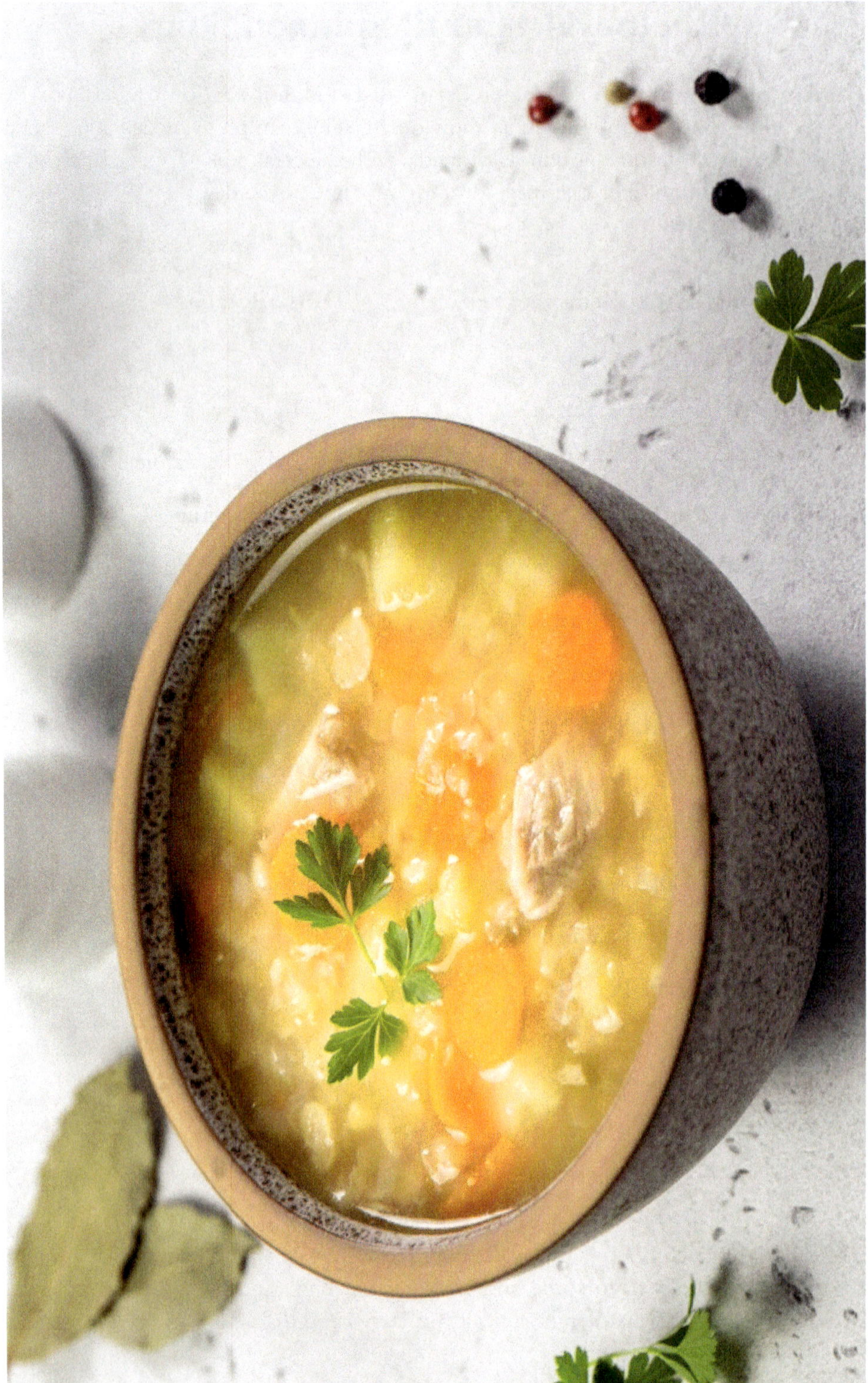

Recipe 45: Split Pea Turkey Soup

Delight in the homely comfort of Split Pea Turkey Soup, a nourishing slow cooker dish perfect for anyone seeking a hearty and satisfying meal. This recipe beautifully combines the richness of turkey with the earthiness of split peas, creating a soup that's filling and packed with flavor and nutrition.

Servings: 1

Prepping Time: 15 minutes

Cook Time: 8 hours

Difficulty: Easy

Ingredients:

- ½ cup dried split peas, rinsed
- 1 small turkey leg or thigh
- 1 carrot, diced
- 1 celery stalk, diced
- ½ onion, chopped
- 1 garlic clove, minced
- 2 cups chicken or turkey broth
- ½ tsp dried thyme
- Salt and pepper to taste

Step-by-Step Preparation:

1. Place split peas, turkey leg, carrot, celery, onion, and garlic in the slow cooker.
2. Pour in the broth.
3. Add dried thyme, salt, and pepper.
4. Cover and cook on low for 8 hours until peas are soft and turkey is cooked through.
5. Remove the turkey, shred the meat, and return it to the soup.
6. Adjust seasoning and serve hot.

Nutritional Facts: (Per serving)

- Calories: 400
- Carbohydrates: 40g
- Protein: 35g
- Fat: 10g
- Saturated Fat: 3g
- Cholesterol: 70mg
- Sodium: 900mg
- Fiber: 16g
- Sugar: 6g

This Split Pea Turkey Soup is a beautiful blend of simplicity and flavor, making it an excellent choice for a comforting and effortless meal. It's the ideal dish for those colder days or whenever you need a warming, nutritious boost.

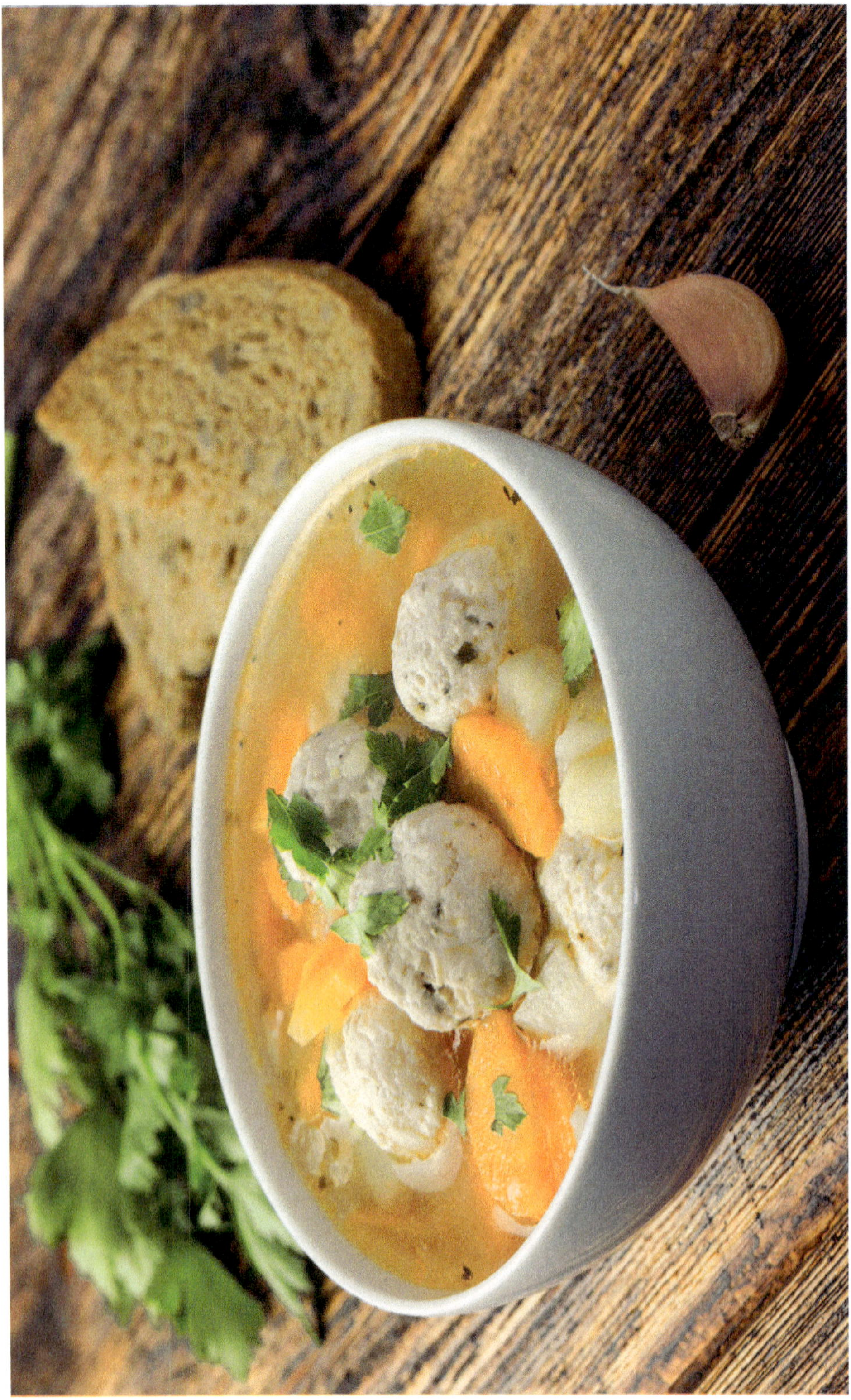

Recipe 46: Meatball Vegetable Soup

Satisfy your cravings for a hearty meal with Meatball Vegetable Soup, a delicious slow cooker dish that combines the comforting flavors of meatballs with a bounty of nutritious vegetables. This one-serving recipe is perfect for those seeking a warm, wholesome meal that's easy to prepare and flavorful, making it an ideal choice for a nourishing solo dinner.

Servings: 1

Prepping Time: 15 minutes

Cook Time: 6 hours

Difficulty: Easy

Ingredients:

- 5 pre-cooked meatballs
- 1 cup mixed vegetables (carrots, peas, corn)
- ½ cup diced tomatoes
- ½ onion, chopped
- 1 garlic clove, minced
- 2 cups beef or vegetable broth
- ½ tsp dried basil
- ½ tsp dried oregano
- Salt and pepper to taste

Step-by-Step Preparation:

1. Place meatballs, mixed vegetables, diced tomatoes, onion, and garlic in the slow cooker.
2. Pour in the broth.
3. Add basil, oregano, salt, and pepper.
4. Stir to combine.
5. Cover and cook on low for 6 hours until vegetables are tender.
6. Adjust seasoning to taste.
7. Serve hot and enjoy.

Nutritional Facts: (Per serving)

- Calories: 320
- Carbohydrates: 25g
- Protein: 20g
- Fat: 16g
- Saturated Fat: 6g
- Cholesterol: 40mg
- Sodium: 900mg
- Fiber: 5g
- Sugar: 8g

Indulge in the rich and savory taste of this Meatball Vegetable Soup, a perfect blend of meatiness and garden-fresh goodness. It's an ideal solution for a hassle-free, delicious meal that warms the heart and satisfies the taste buds.

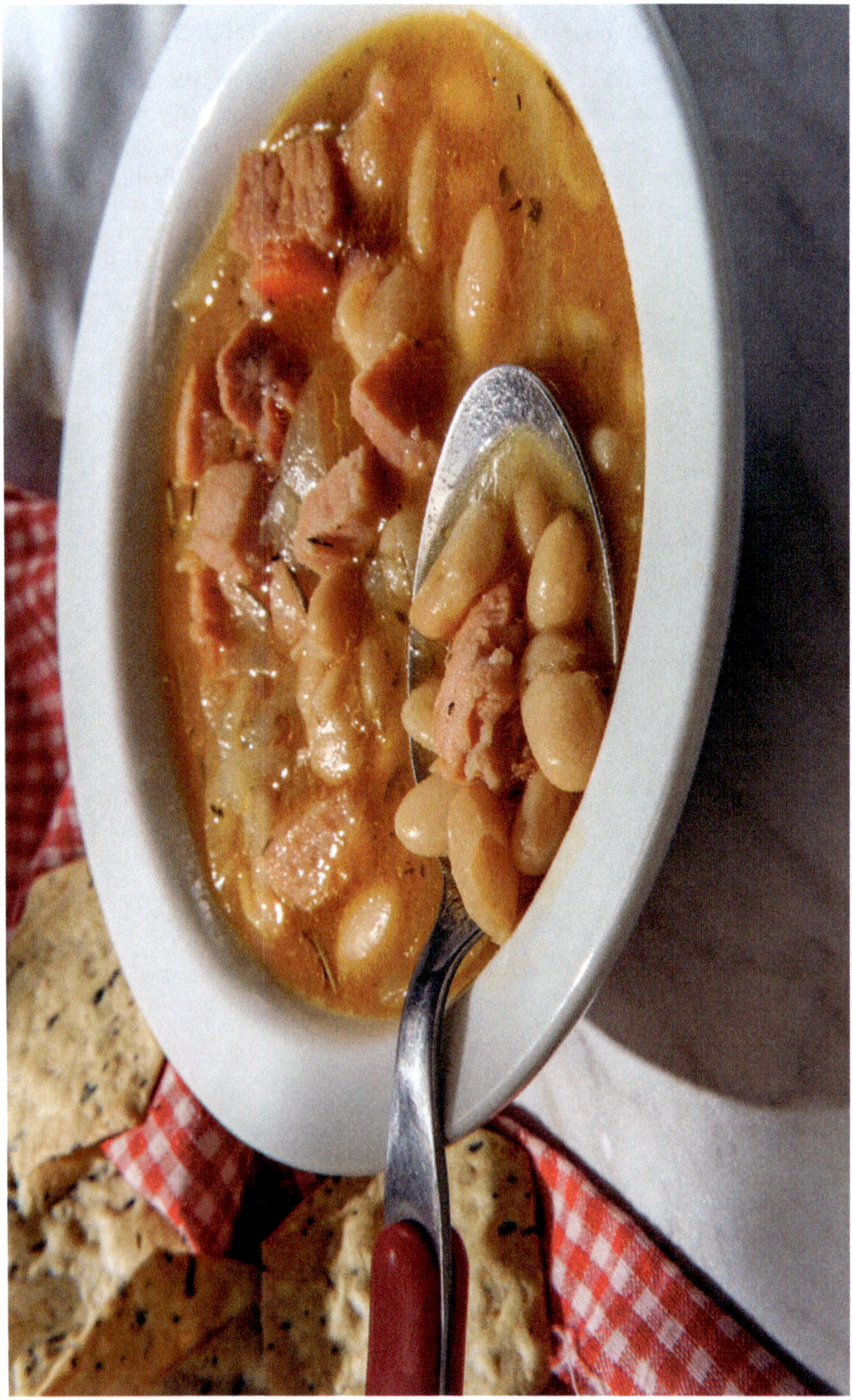

Recipe 47: Ham and Cannellini Bean Soup

Indulge in the comfort of a warm, hearty Ham and Cannellini Bean Soup bowl. This slow cooker recipe is perfect for a nourishing meal that combines the savory flavors of ham with the creamy texture of cannellini beans.

Servings: 1

Prepping Time: 15 minutes

Cook Time: 6 hours

Difficulty: Easy

Ingredients:

- 1/2 cup diced ham
- 1/2 can cannellini beans, drained and rinsed
- 1 carrot, chopped
- 1/2 onion, diced
- 1 clove garlic, minced
- 2 cups chicken broth
- 1/2 teaspoon dried thyme
- Salt and pepper, to taste

Step-by-Step Preparation:

1. Place the diced ham, cannellini beans, carrot, onion, and garlic into the slow cooker.
2. Pour in the chicken broth, ensuring all ingredients are covered.
3. Add dried thyme, salt, and pepper.
4. Stir gently to combine.
5. Set the slow cooker low for 6 hours until the vegetables are tender.

Nutritional Facts: (Per serving)

- Calories: 320
- Protein: 25g
- Carbohydrates: 40g
- Fat: 8g
- Sodium: 870mg
- Fiber: 9g

Savor each spoonful of this delicious Ham and Cannellini Bean Soup. Perfect for a cozy night in, this one-serving slow cooker recipe is easy to make and packed with flavor and nutrients. Enjoy the simplicity and warmth it brings to your table!

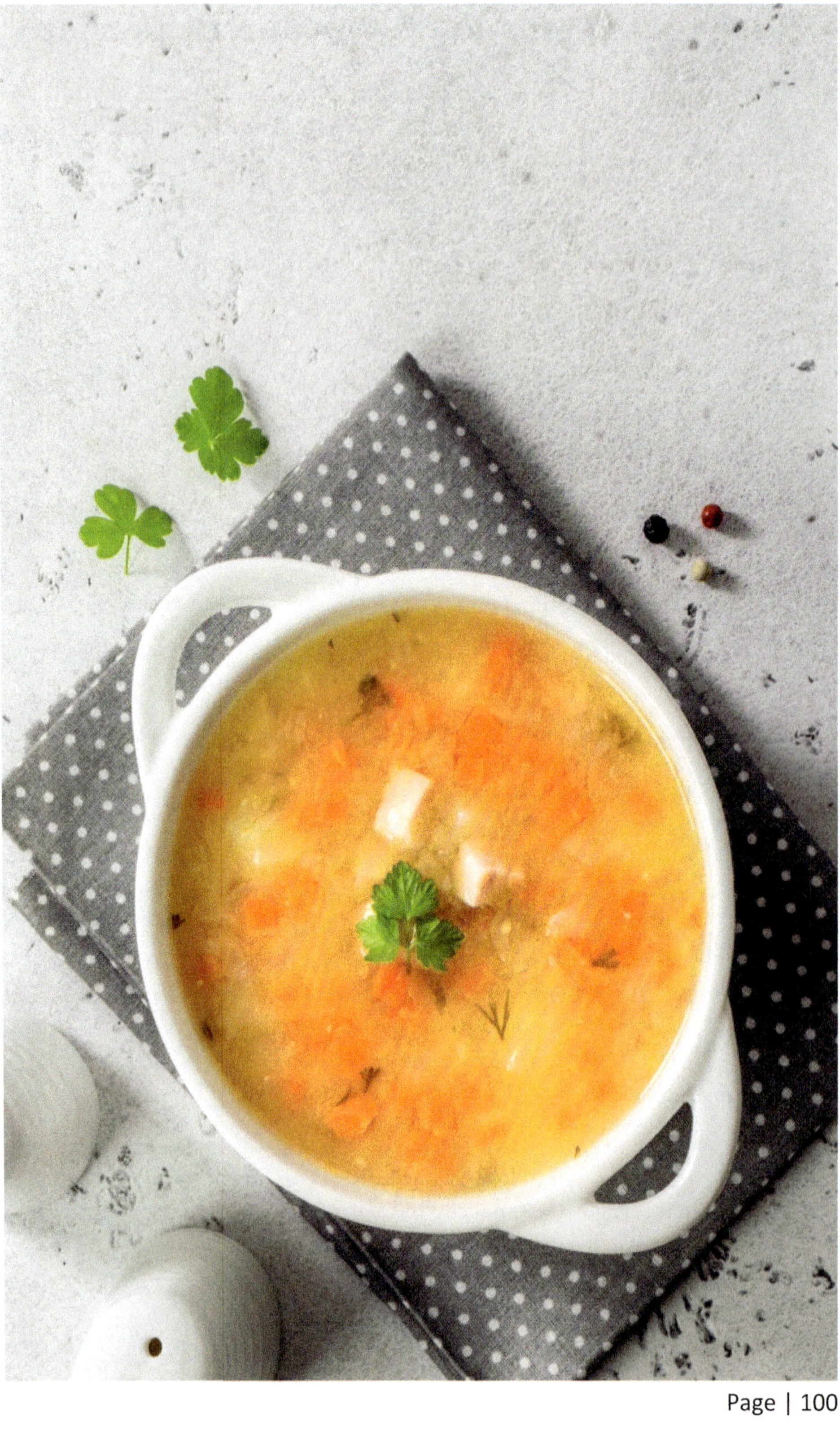

Recipe 48: Split Pea Bacon Soup

Experience the rich and smoky flavors of Split Pea Bacon Soup, a delightful slow cooker dish designed for one. This recipe perfectly combines tender split peas and savory bacon for a comforting meal that's effortless to prepare.

Servings: 1

Cook Time: 8 hours

Prepping Time: 10 minutes

Difficulty: Easy

Ingredients:

- 1/2 cup dried split peas
- 2 slices bacon, chopped
- 1/4 onion, diced
- 1 small carrot, chopped
- 1/4 teaspoon dried thyme
- 2 cups chicken or vegetable broth
- Salt and pepper, to taste

Step-by-Step Preparation:

1. Rinse and drain the split peas.
2. Place them in the slow cooker with the chopped bacon, onion, carrot, and thyme.
3. Pour in the broth, then season with salt and pepper.
4. Stir to mix the ingredients.
5. Cover and cook on low for 8 hours, until the peas are soft and the soup has thickened.

Nutritional Facts: (Per serving)

- Calories: 310
- Protein: 19g
- Carbohydrates: 45g
- Fat: 7g
- Sodium: 980mg
- Fiber: 16g

Dive into the wholesome goodness of this Split Pea Bacon Soup. Whether you're looking for a simple, satisfying meal or a new addition to your slow cooker repertoire, this one-serving soup is an ideal choice for a hassle-free, delicious experience.

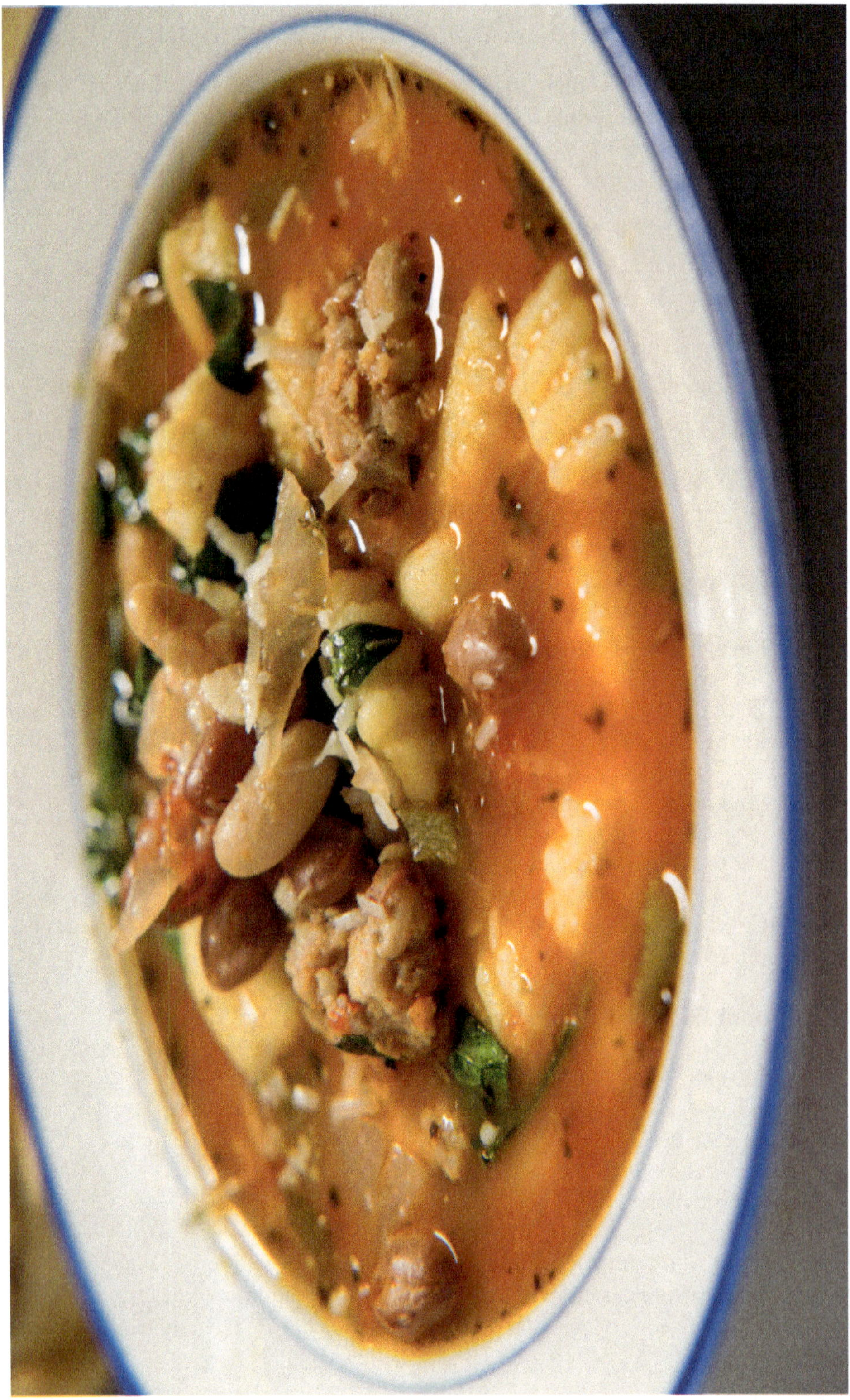

Recipe 49: Tuscany Sausage Gnocchi Bean Soup

Delight in the rustic flavors of Italy with this Tuscany Sausage Gnocchi Bean Soup, a one-pot wonder crafted for a single serving. This slow cooker recipe effortlessly combines savory sausage, hearty beans, and pillow gnocchi, creating a soup that's as comforting as it is flavorful.

Servings: 1

Prepping Time: 15 minutes

Cook Time: 6 hours

Difficulty: Easy

Ingredients:

- 1 Italian sausage, sliced
- 1/2 cup canned cannellini beans, drained
- 1/2 cup gnocchi
- 1/4 cup chopped spinach
- 1/2 tomato, diced
- 1 garlic clove, minced
- 2 cups vegetable broth
- 1/4 teaspoon Italian seasoning
- Salt and pepper, to taste

Step-by-Step Preparation:

1. Brown the sausage slices in a pan over medium heat, then transfer to the slow cooker.
2. Add cannellini beans, gnocchi, chopped spinach, diced tomato, and minced garlic to the cooker.
3. Pour in the vegetable broth.
4. Sprinkle with Italian seasoning, salt, and pepper.
5. Stir gently to combine.
6. Cover and cook on low for 6 hours, until gnocchi is tender and flavors meld.

Nutritional Facts: (Per serving)

- Calories: 450
- Protein: 25g
- Carbohydrates: 45g
- Fat: 20g
- Sodium: 1200mg
- Fiber: 6g

Savor the essence of Tuscany with this Sausage Gnocchi Bean Soup, a delightful blend of traditional Italian ingredients in a simple yet delicious one-serving meal. Perfect for a cozy night, this slow cooker soup promises to warm your heart and tantalize your taste buds.

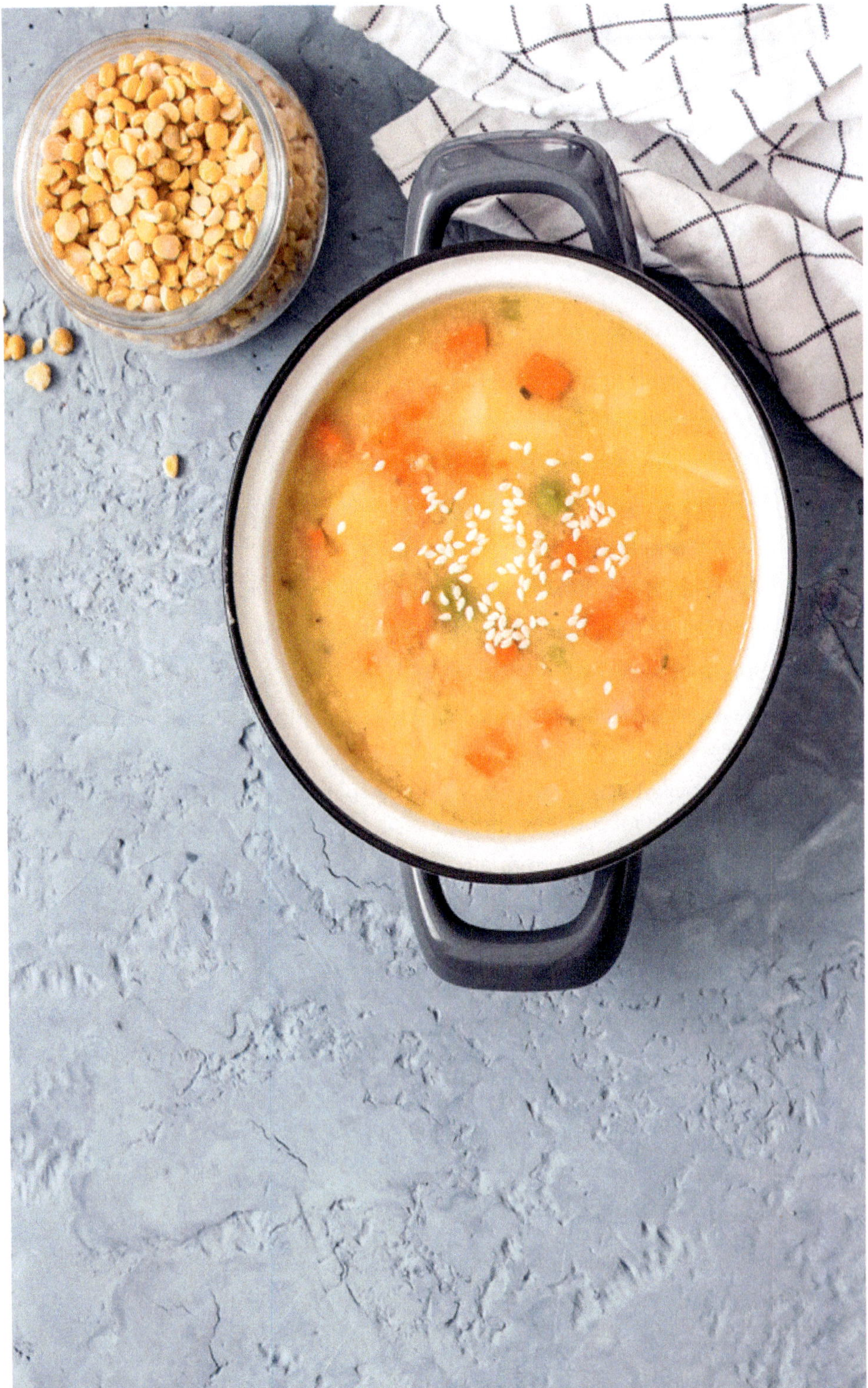

Recipe 50: Sweet Potato Split Pea Soup

Immerse yourself in the wholesome and comforting flavors of Sweet Potato Split Pea Soup. This slow cooker recipe, perfect for one, beautifully marries the natural sweetness of sweet potatoes with the earthy tones of split peas, creating a nourishing and heartwarming meal.

Servings: 1

Prepping Time: 10 minutes

Cook Time: 8 hours

Difficulty: Easy

Ingredients:

- 1/2 cup dried split peas
- 1/2 large sweet potato, peeled and diced
- 1/4 onion, chopped
- 1 small carrot, chopped
- 1/2 teaspoon garlic powder
- 2 cups vegetable broth
- 1/4 teaspoon smoked paprika
- Salt and pepper, to taste

Step-by-Step Preparation:

1. Rinse the split peas and place them in the slow cooker.
2. Add the diced sweet potato, chopped onion, and carrot.
3. Sprinkle with garlic powder, smoked paprika, salt, and pepper.
4. Pour in the vegetable broth, ensuring all ingredients are submerged.
5. Stir gently to mix.
6. Cover and cook on low for 8 hours, until peas and potatoes are tender.

Nutritional Facts: (Per serving)

- Calories: 330
- Protein: 18g
- Carbohydrates: 62g
- Fat: 1g
- Sodium: 480mg
- Fiber: 21g

Relish in the simplicity and depth of flavors of this Sweet Potato Split Pea Soup. A perfect dish for those seeking a healthy, satisfying meal, it's an easy-to-make slow cooker recipe that offers comfort in every spoonful, ideal for a cozy, relaxing evening.

Conclusion

As we turn the final page of "Solo Slow Cooking: Effortless One-Person Meals with Easy Steps," it's clear that this journey through the art of slow cooking has been more than just about preparing meals for one. Diana Stone has masterfully presented a cookbook that simplifies the cooking process with the slow cooker and enriches the solo dining experience with flavors, textures, and colors that delight the senses. Through 50 authentic recipes spread across five diverse chapters—Meat, Chicken, Vegetarian, Fish, Seafood, Soup—this book has offered a culinary adventure tailored to individual tastes and preferences.

Celebrating Solo Culinary Adventures

"Solo Slow Cooking" has been a testament to the joy and fulfillment of cooking for oneself. Each recipe, accompanied by vibrant photos, serves as a guide and a visual inspiration, encouraging even the most novice cooks to explore the richness of flavors that can be achieved with a slow cooker. The standard color printing enhances these images, making every recipe a visual feast as much as a culinary one.

Empowering the Individual Cook

Diana Stone's approachable instructions have made slow cooking accessible to everyone, ensuring perfect flavors are within reach, regardless of one's cooking expertise. The meticulous attention to detail, from the selection of ingredients to the clarity of each step, ensures a successful outcome every time, fostering a sense of confidence and creativity in the kitchen.

A Lasting Impression

"Solo Slow Cooking" leaves us with more than just recipes; it provides a new perspective on the possibilities of solo dining. The book underscores the importance of treating oneself to nourishing and indulgent meals, turning everyday dining into an occasion to look forward to. The absence of grammatical or spelling errors further elevates the reading experience, allowing the focus to remain on the joy of cooking and the pleasure of savoring each dish.

In conclusion, "Solo Slow Cooking: Effortless One-Person Meals with Easy Steps" is more than a cookbook—it's a companion for those who cherish the process of cooking and the intimacy of enjoying a meal made just for oneself. Diana Stone has crafted a guide that inspires, empowers, and delights, proving that solo cooking can be a rewarding and flavorful adventure. As we close this book, let's carry forward the inspiration it has provided, exploring new recipes and embracing the art of solo slow cooking with enthusiasm and confidence.

Printed in Great Britain
by Amazon